# WISDOM

*from*

# RICK

# JOYNER

# OTHER BOOKS BY RICK JOYNER

*The Journey Begins (Divine Destiny Series)*

*There Were Two Trees in the Garden (Divine Destiny Series)*

*The Prophetic Ministry*

*The Call*

*The Final Quest*

*The Torch and the Sword*

*Forgiveness: Mobilizing a Power-Filled Life*

*Leadership Development: Keys to Advancement*

*Overcoming Evil in the Last Days*

*Delivered From Evil: Preparing for the Age to Come*

*Breaking the Power of Evil (Expanded)*

*Understanding the Times*

*The Overcoming Life*

*Leadership: The Power of a Creative Life*

*Overcoming the Religious Spirit (Combating Spiritual Strongholds Series)*

*Overcoming Witchcraft (Combating Spiritual Strongholds Series)*

*Overcoming the Accuser (Combating Spiritual Strongholds Series)*

*Overcoming the Spirit of Poverty (Combating Spiritual Strongholds Series)*

*Overcoming Fear (Combating Spiritual Strongholds Series)*

*Overcoming Confusion (Combating Spiritual Strongholds Series)*

*Fire That Could Not Die (Hall of Faith Series)*

*A Message to the Glorious Church:*
*A Verse by Verse Study of Ephesians Chapters 1-4*

*A Message to the Glorious Church:*
*A Verse by Verse Study of Ephesians Chapters 5-6*

*The Power to Change the World*

*Epic Battles of the Last Days*

*The Apostolic Ministry*

*Breaking the Power of Evil: Winning the Battle for the Soul of Man*

*Visions of the Harvest*

AVAILABLE FROM DESTINY IMAGE PUBLISHERS

# WISDOM
*from*
# RICK
# JOYNER

*Rick Joyner*

Compiled by Angela Rickabaugh Shears

DESTINY IMAGE® PUBLISHERS, INC.

P.O. Box 310, Shippensburg, PA 17257-0310

*"Speaking to the Purposes of God for This Generation and for the Generations to Come."*

This book and all other Destiny Image, Revival Press, MercyPlace, Fresh Bread, Destiny Image Fiction, and Treasure House books are available at Christian bookstores and distributors worldwide.

For a U.S. bookstore nearest you, call **1-800-722-6774.**

For more information on foreign distributors, call **717-532-3040.**

Reach us on the Internet: **www.destinyimage.com.**

International Trade Paper ISBN 13: 978-0-7684-3287-9

Hardcover ISBN 978-0-7684-3255-8

Large Print ISBN 978-0-7684-3451-4

Ebook ISBN 978-0-7684-9114-2

For Worldwide Distribution, Printed in the U.S.A.

1 2 3 4 5 6 7 8 9 10 / 14 13 12 11 10

# Contents

Introduction . . . . . . . . . . . . . . . . . . . . . . . . . . . . . . . . . . . . . . . . . . . . .7

1    Wisdom's Path . . . . . . . . . . . . . . . . . . . . . . . . . . . . . . . . . . . . . . .9

2    Wisdom of Freedom. . . . . . . . . . . . . . . . . . . . . . . . . . . . . . . . . . 15

3    Wisdom's Authority . . . . . . . . . . . . . . . . . . . . . . . . . . . . . . . . . . 21

4    Wisdom Weaponry. . . . . . . . . . . . . . . . . . . . . . . . . . . . . . . . . . . 29

5    Wisdom and Peace . . . . . . . . . . . . . . . . . . . . . . . . . . . . . . . . . . . 35

6    Wisdom Over Poverty. . . . . . . . . . . . . . . . . . . . . . . . . . . . . . . . . 41

7    Wisdom of Learning From Mistakes . . . . . . . . . . . . . . . . . . . . . . 49

8    Wisdom Thwarts Evil. . . . . . . . . . . . . . . . . . . . . . . . . . . . . . . . . . 57

9    Wisdom Against Idols . . . . . . . . . . . . . . . . . . . . . . . . . . . . . . . . . 63

10   Wisdom to Escape the Wilderness . . . . . . . . . . . . . . . . . . . . . . . 71

11   Wisdom of Fear. . . . . . . . . . . . . . . . . . . . . . . . . . . . . . . . . . . . . . 79

12   Wisdom to Change . . . . . . . . . . . . . . . . . . . . . . . . . . . . . . . . . . 85

13   Wisdom of God's Heart . . . . . . . . . . . . . . . . . . . . . . . . . . . . . . . 91

14   Wisdom and Truth. . . . . . . . . . . . . . . . . . . . . . . . . . . . . . . . . . . 97

15   Wisdom Versus Idealism . . . . . . . . . . . . . . . . . . . . . . . . . . . . . . 105

16   Wisdom Beyond Human Ability . . . . . . . . . . . . . . . . . . . . . . . . 111

17   Wisdom and Miracles . . . . . . . . . . . . . . . . . . . . . . . . . . . . . . . . 119

18   Wisdom of Democracy . . . . . . . . . . . . . . . . . . . . . . . . . . . . . . . 127

19   Wisdom to Destroy Racism . . . . . . . . . . . . . . . . . . . . . . . . . . . . 135

| 20 | Wisdom and Love | 143 |
|----|-----------------|-----|
| 21 | Wisdom Over Witchcraft | 151 |
| 22 | Wisdom Over a Religious Spirit | 159 |
| 23 | Wisdom's Ultimate Battle | 165 |
| 24 | Wisdom, Redemption, and Restoration | 171 |
| 25 | Wisdom Overcomes Rebellion | 177 |
| 26 | Wisdom, Not Confusion | 183 |
| 27 | Wisdom and Trust | 189 |
| 28 | Wisdom to Meet Needs | 195 |
| 29 | Wisdom Over Pride | 201 |
| 30 | Wisdom's Light | 207 |
| 31 | Wisdom of Life | 213 |
| 32 | Wisdom of Diversity | 219 |
| 33 | Wisdom of Marriage | 225 |
| 34 | Wisdom and Communication | 231 |
| 35 | Wisdom, Not Jealousy | 237 |
| 36 | Wisdom, Sacrifice, and the Cross | 245 |
| 37 | Wisdom to Dream of Heaven | 253 |
| 38 | Wisdom of the Holy Spirit | 259 |
| 39 | Wisdom and Loyalty | 267 |
| 40 | Wisdom's Love | 273 |
|    | Endnotes | 281 |

# Introduction

*How much better it is to get wisdom than gold!*
*And to get understanding is to be chosen above silver*
(Proverbs 16:16).

**W**ISDOM *From Rick Joyner* is a compilation of wisdom received from the Lord over many years of serving Him. Shared with you are 40 personal insights to strengthen and inspire you to tackle life's challenges, rejoice in God's promises fulfilled, and shout victory over the enemy. Excerpts of wisdom are gleaned from the following popular books by best-selling author Rick Joyner: *High Calling; Delivered From Evil; Unshakable Faith; Overcoming Evil in the Last Days; An Enduring Vision;* and *Breaking the Power of Evil.*[1]

This interactive devotional journal immerses you into a world where God's powerful wisdom infuses you with the richness of His love and mercy. You will be empowered to solve problems, turn situations around, and make wise decisions.

As Joyner writes in his book, *Delivered From Evil*:

One of the most devastating ploys of the devil has been to get Christians to develop theologies and beliefs from wounds, rejections, and failures rather than from the Scriptures.[2]

Within each chapter are truth-filled Scriptures, wise reflections from best-selling books, and provocative "Points to Ponder" that will help you to delve into the depths of yourself to search out things, issues, people, situations, and "other stuff" that you need to deal with to be able to move forward toward your God-given destiny.

"Words of Wisdom" from other well-known believers will cause you to consider various points of view about important life-changing topics.

And located at the end of each chapter, "My Wisdom Keys" is a place for your own special thoughts, a place to record your heart's desires, feelings, ideas, wonderings, and inner yearnings.

This treasured keepsake will launch you into a spiritual realm filled with wisdom and paved with God's glory.

# 1

# *Wisdom's Path*

Wisdom is the ability to apply knowledge properly. In Proverbs 24:3-4 we are told, *"By wisdom a house is built, and by understanding it is established; and by knowledge the rooms are filled with all precious and pleasant riches."* It is true that sermons filled with knowledge will tend to draw people. The gift of a word of knowledge will also draw crowds. This is good, but our purpose in the Lord is not just to draw crowds, but also to see people built together into the house of the Lord. To do this we need wisdom.

[The following excerpts are adapted from *High Calling.*]

# Wisdom's Path Reflections

THE gift of a word of wisdom may not be as spectacular as the gift of a word of knowledge, but it is every bit as essential for the work of God to be accomplished.

How do we acquire wisdom? We just need to ask, as we are told in James 1:5: *"But if any of you lacks wisdom, let him ask of God, who gives to all generously and without reproach, and it will be given to him."* It is wisdom to understand that we need wisdom. This is a fundamental humility, which is a prerequisite for wisdom, as we read in Proverbs 11:2: *"When pride comes, then comes dishonor, but with the humble is wisdom."*

A basic characteristic of humility is teachableness. A tragic pride has gripped our souls when others cannot teach us. The depth of our humility might be demonstrated by how open we are to being taught by those whom we might consider inferior. Was this not the great test, and the reason why the Lord, who was Wisdom Himself, came as a humble carpenter? Is this not why He called the *"uneducated and untrained"* (Acts 4:13) to be His apostles?

It seems that He so structured His ministry and His Church to filter out the proud and attract only the humble. We can see that this is basic to the Lord's nature in James 4:6 and First Peter 5:5, which both state that *"God is opposed to the proud, but gives grace to the humble."*

Knowledge fills our lives, but wisdom builds them. Therefore, in the building of our lives, families, churches, and ministries, the seeking of wisdom must be a priority. To do this, we must seek humility. It is therefore wise to associate with the lowly, and learn to patiently listen to those whom we may be prone to think are inferior.

The Lord Jesus Himself rejoiced saying, *"I praise You, Father, Lord of heaven and earth, that You have hidden these things from the wise and intelligent and have revealed them to infants"* (Matt. 11:25). He also said that we would have to become like little children to enter the Kingdom. One of the basic characteristics of children is that they are teachable. Humility is the way that the Kingdom will come to our lives.

# *Points to Ponder*

The depth of your humility might be demonstrated by how open you are to being taught by those whom you might consider inferior.

Was this not the great test, and the reason why the Lord, who was Wisdom Himself, came as a humble carpenter?

Knowledge fills your life, but wisdom builds it.

In the building of your life, family, church, and ministry, the seeking of wisdom must be a priority. To do this, you must seek humility.

You are wise to associate with the lowly, and learn to patiently listen to those whom you may think are inferior.

# *Words of Wisdom*

*For the Lord gives wisdom; from His mouth come knowledge and understanding* (Proverbs 2:6).

It should fill us with joy, that infinite wisdom guides the affairs of the world. Many of its events are shrouded in darkness and mystery, and inextricable confusion sometimes seems to reign. Often wickedness prevails, and God seems to have forgotten the creatures that he has made. Our own path through life is dark and devious, and beset with difficulties and dangers. How full of consolation is the doctrine, that infinite wisdom directs every event, brings order out of confusion, and light out of darkness, and, to those who love God, causes all things, whatever be their present aspect and apparent tendency, to work together for good.

—J.L. Dagg, *Manual of Theology*[1]

Let us touch the dying, the poor, the lonely and the unwanted according to the graces we have received and let us not be ashamed or slow to do the humble work.

—Mother Teresa

# MY WISDOM KEYS

_____

_____

_____

_____

_____

_____

_____

_____

_____

_____

_____

_____

_____

# 2

## *Wisdom of Freedom*

God created man to be free. We cannot be who we were created to be without freedom. If all that the Lord wanted was perfect, harmonious worship, He would have done better to create computers instead of humans so He could just program them to worship Him in perfect harmony. Certainly our God is worthy of more than that, but in order to have more than that, there must be freedom.

In the domain of darkness there is fear, oppression, and bondage. In the Kingdom of God there is faith and freedom.

[The following excerpts are adapted from *Breaking the Power of Evil.*]

# Wisdom of Freedom Reflections

FUNDAMENTAL to understanding the truth is understanding that man was created to be a free moral agent. This does not in any way infringe on the sovereignty of God; rather, it illuminates His sovereignty. The greatest, most noble authority is always demonstrated by the freedom it allows its subjects. The Lord wants us to worship Him and reject evil because we love Him and love His truth, not just because we are afraid of punishment. There are consequences for disobedience that we cannot overlook, yes, but our main goal must be to obey because we love God and because He is worthy of our devotion.

Freedom involves choices that we must make. With our choices there are consequences. This means that with freedom comes responsibility. Why? Man is called to rule with God, and there can be no true authority without a corresponding responsibility. So the greater the authority is, the greater the potential for good when making the right choice—but also the greater potential for bad when we make the wrong one. Because Adam was given authority over the whole world, when he fell the whole world suffered. To the degree that we are given authority, we also can release good or evil into that domain.

The Lord came to save us from our sin. When Jesus prayed for His people on the night before His crucifixion, He said concerning us, *"As You sent Me into the world, I also have sent them into the world"* (John 17:18). So we are sent for the same basic purpose that He was—to destroy the works of the devil. That is why we are on the earth—to be His Body through which He can continue His work.

Every Christian is called to be a freedom fighter—to set the captives free, to see every human soul set free of bondage to the devil and released into the glorious liberty of the children of God. Because of this, the love of freedom must be basic to our spiritual genetic code.

Every soul that is set free is a victory that conquers more territory for the Kingdom of God. Even so, we must look beyond setting just individuals free and look toward setting whole nations free from the bondage they are in, in this present evil age.

# *Points to Ponder*

What does being a "free moral agent" mean to you?

The Lord wants you to worship Him and reject evil because you love Him and love His truth, not just because you are afraid of punishment.

The greater the authority, the greater the potential for good when making the right choice—but also the greater potential for bad when you make the wrong choice.

You, Christian, are called to be a freedom fighter—to set captives free to be released into the glorious liberty of His grace and mercy.

# *Words of Wisdom*

The Governor, the Holy Spirit, is the Master Gardener who ensures that the gardens of our lives produce good fruit that is appropriate and pleasing to the King, to whom the gardens belong. Could there be any greater freedom—or any greater destiny—than this?

—Myles Munroe, *Wisdom From Myles Munroe*[1]

When the infirm woman came to Jesus, He proclaimed her freedom. When He did, she stood erect for the first time in 18 years. When you come to Jesus, He will cause you to stand in His power, His anointing.

—T.D. Jakes, *Power for Living*[2]

True liberty consists only in the power of doing what we ought to will, and in not being constrained to do what we ought not to will.

—Jonathan Edwards

"I'm healed!" Then Irene ran to her neighbor's pool, jumped in, and began swimming! She was ecstatic because she was performing movements that had been impossible for her.

—Ché Ahn, *Say Goodbye to Powerless Christianity*[3]

19

# MY WISDOM KEYS

_____

_____

_____

_____

_____

_____

_____

_____

_____

_____

_____

_____

_____

_____

# 3

## Wisdom's Authority

As Christians we have a different mandate of authority. We are not here in this age to avenge evil, but in fact are required to love our enemies and pray for them. Our warfare is not against people, but against whatever has people in bondage. The greatest victory of all would be the repentance and salvation of our enemies.

Many Christians have a difficult time understanding the two different mandates given to civil governments and to the Church. However, this is something important that we must settle in our hearts if we are going to be effective in our job of tearing down the spiritual strongholds that keep people in bondage.

[The following excerpts are adapted from *Breaking the Power of Evil*.]

# Wisdom's Authority Reflections

OUR civil governments are fighting a righteous war against evil as they combat terrorism or governments that promote terrorism. Even so, the Church is called to a much different battle. We are called to fight the unseen war that is being waged in the heavenly places. Ours is a spiritual war.

This does not mean that Christians cannot join the military forces of nations to fight the war on the level of civil authority. However, they should understand that while marching under the orders of civil governments, their authority will be exercised through their physical weapons, not their spiritual ones. This does not mean that Christian soldiers should not pray and try to use their spiritual authority too, but when you're in battle, don't drop your gun to do so! If you are under orders from a civil government, you must not hesitate to use the weapons that the government has given to you for fighting.

Likewise, if we are operating under the mandate given to the Church, we do not have authority to use the weapons that are used for fighting flesh and blood for our battle. This is why "Christian militias" that arm themselves with guns or other physical weapons will always be motivated by fear and paranoia. They are actually controlled by evil since they are not properly under either of the mandates of authority that God has given to men.

Spiritual authority is something that we grow into. We are given more authority as we mature spiritually and are given higher commissions by the Lord. This will be evidenced by an increase of faith to new levels. We see in the Book of Acts that Paul the apostle was called as an apostle many years before he was actually commissioned to that ministry. With that commissioning came authority on a higher level.

Being called to a high position does not automatically give one authority. Maturity and the faithfulness that goes on to possess the promises is what will release true authority in us. However, we must understand that spiritual authority is not given so that we get more respect from people, but so we can fight effectively against the powers that are destroying people.

# *Points to Ponder*

You are called to fight, with wisdom and authority, the unseen war that is being waged in the heavenly places.

Christian soldiers should pray and use their spiritual authority.

You are given more authority as you mature spiritually and are given higher commissions by the Lord.

You will experience an increase of your faith to new levels when given more authority.

Maturity and the faithfulness that go on to possess the promises are what will release true authority in you.

# *Words of Wisdom*

Authority and responsibility always go together and we must understand both of these aspects of our call. God has invested His church with His authority over everything on earth, but we also have the responsibility to use that authority to fulfill His purposes.

—Kris Vallotton and Bill Johnson
*The Supernatural Ways of Royalty*[1]

Christ has entrusted within the lives of all true believers the same mighty power and authority that resides in His name. When you intercede and pray in the power and authority that is in Jesus' name, you will be able to ask anything whatsoever you will and He will do it!

—Morris Cerullo, *How to Pray*[2]

*And Jesus came up and spoke to them, saying, "All authority has been given to Me in heaven and on earth. Go therefore and make disciples of all the nations, baptizing them in the name of the Father and the Son and the Holy Spirit, teaching them to observe all that I commanded you; and lo, I am with you always, even to the end of the age"* (Matthew 28:18-20).

The fundamental basis of all Christian missionary enterprise is the universal authority of Jesus Christ, "in heaven and on earth." If the authority of Jesus were circumscribed on earth, if He were but one of many religious teachers, one of many Jewish prophets, one of many divine incarnations, we would have no mandate to present Him to the nations as the Lord and Savior of the world. If the authority of Jesus were limited in heaven, if He has not decisively overthrown the principalities and powers, we might still proclaim Him to the nations, but we would never be able to *turn them from darkness to light, and from the power of Satan unto God*" (Acts 26:18 KJV). Only because all authority on earth belongs to Christ dare we go to all nations. And only because all authority in heaven as well is His have we any hope of success.

—John Stott, "The Great Commission,"
in *One Race, One Gospel, One Task*[3]

## MY WISDOM KEYS

_____

_____

_____

_____

_____

_____

_____

_____

_____

_____

_____

_____

_____

_____

_____
_____
_____
_____
_____
_____
_____
_____
_____
_____
_____
_____
_____
_____
_____
_____
_____
_____
_____
_____

# 4

# *Wisdom Weaponry*

It may seem like another paradox, but we cannot function properly as part of this great army that we are called to be until we are firmly established in the peace of God. One of the most powerful spiritual weapons that has been given to God's people is peace. We may think that peace is not a weapon, but in actuality, it is such a powerful weapon that in Romans 16:20, Paul did not write that it was the Lord of hosts, or the Lord of armies who would crush the enemy, but that *"the **God of peace** will soon crush Satan under your feet"* (Rom. 16:20). When we abide in the peace of God, it is both a fortress and a weapon that the enemy has no power against.

[The following excerpts are adapted from *Breaking the Power of Evil*.]

# Wisdom Weaponry Reflections

IF we abide in the peace of God in a situation, it unravels the enemy's power over that situation. That is why most attacks of the enemy upon believers are intended to first rob them of their peace. The peace of God is the linchpin fruit of the Spirit that must be in place in order to hold all the others in their places. Once we lose the peace of God, we quickly lose our patience, love, self-control, etc. This causes us to fall from our position of abiding in Christ. If we are truly abiding in Christ, the fruit of the Spirit will always demonstrate it.

Because we represent the Prince of Peace and because it is the peacemakers who are called the *"sons of God"* (Matt. 5:9), it is the Church that the world should be turning to for the solutions to its conflicts. Our victory over evil is accomplished by overcoming it with good. We destroy the enemy's power of destruction by standing in and imparting peace.

However, instead of the world turning to the Church for solutions to its conflicts, the Church is now viewed more as a source of conflicts. This will change. The Church is called to judge the world, and as conflicts and anxiety grow in the world, peace and wisdom are going to grow in the Church to such an extent that even the heathen will start coming to Christians for help. Through this the Church's spiritual authority will grow stronger and stronger as lawlessness erodes human authority.

The Church is the *"Jerusalem above,"* the spiritual Jerusalem that Paul mentions in Galatians 4:26. *Jerusalem* means "city of peace." Like the earthly Jerusalem, the Church is now embroiled in almost continuous strife with war within herself as well as war against the forces of the world without. Even so, she soon will be victorious over the strife within, and then she will be able to turn all her great weapons on the forces without. When she does, she will bring peace in place of conflict.

Peace will be one of the greatest witnesses (weapons) of the Lord in the midst of His people. It is through abiding in His peace that we will be able to crush every manifestation of the enemy in our life. Peace itself is the victory.

# *Points to Ponder*

If you abide in the peace of God in a situation, it unravels the enemy's power over that situation.

Most attacks of the enemy upon believers are intended to first rob you of your peace.

The peace of God is the linchpin fruit of the Spirit that must be in place in order to hold all the others in their places.

When you lose the peace of God, you quickly lose your patience, love, and self-control.

If you are truly abiding in Christ, the fruit of the Spirit will always demonstrate it.

# Words of Wisdom

The punishment from God demonstrates the law of God. Those who reject God in peace hate God all the more when judged by war. Because they won't turn to God in war or peace, the Lawgiver must demonstrate His control, punishing the lawbreaker by immersing him in lawless anguish.

—Elmer L. Towns, *Praying the Book of Revelation*[1]

*Wisdom is better than weapons of war, but one sinner destroys much good* (Ecclesiastes 9:18).

The ultimate weapon to use against those who do evil is to love them: to meet their needs.

—Lou Priolo

But David was full of courage and promptly answered his cocky opponent. Your biggest mistake is to keep silent when the devil is testing you. To win you must declare the final outcome of victory to his face before it manifests, and you have to do it boldly, without hesitation. That is exactly what David did.

—Keith Hudson, *The Cry*[2]

# MY WISDOM KEYS

_____

_____

_____

_____

_____

_____

_____

_____

_____

_____

_____

_____

_____

# 5

## *Wisdom and Peace*

Pride caused the Fall of satan and almost every fall since. We know that *"God is opposed to the proud, but gives grace to the humble"* (James 4:6). Anxiety is a form of pride; it actually asserts that we think the matter is too big for God so we have to handle it ourselves. If we really believe that He is God, however, we will cease striving, cast off our anxiety, and live in the peace that comes from knowing that He is in control.

[The following excerpts are adapted from *Breaking the Power of Evil.*]

# Wisdom and Peace Reflections

IT is no accident that "panic attacks" have now reached epidemic proportions almost throughout the earth. Anxiety is rising dramatically in the world, but peace will rise correspondingly in those who are true followers of Christ. The anxiety that is coming upon the world is the direct result of people trying to live without God and do everything on their own. That is why the original temptation was to get Adam and Eve to try to become what God had in fact called them to be, but to do it without God. Peace can come only by returning to Him.

The more humankind turns from God, the more striving and confusion there will be, which will result in even more fear. This increases impatience, self-centeredness, and other "deeds of the flesh" that cause conflict. Christians must not live as the world lives. We must grow in the knowledge of the Lord's authority and control. We must grow in the peace of God.

When we walk in the peace of God in our home, it will ultimately crush the enemy's influence there. If we walk in the peace of God at work, it will soon crush the enemy's influence there. If the Christians in a city would walk in the peace of God, the Church there would soon come into unity, and the enemy's influence over that city would be crushed. When Christians in any nation truly begin to walk in the peace of God, they will crush the enemy's influence over the nation.

After years of inquiring of the Lord to know what we could do as a ministry for Israel, I was told to send "missionaries of peace" to live there. Their main calling is to walk in the peace and rest of God so that their joy and peace in the midst of the stress would stand out as an oasis in contrast to the spirit now prevailing over that nation. When the believers who live there are delivered of anxiety and begin to walk in the peace of God, it will be the most striking witness of the Prince of Peace that Israel has had since the first century. When this is demonstrated, it will make this peace of the heart even more desirable than peace with the nations around them. There is no peace like the peace of God, and this alone can lead to a true peace among those neighbors.

True peace is the condition of the heart that trusts God regardless of the circumstances.

# *Points to Ponder*

Anxiety is rising dramatically in the world, but peace in you will rise as a true follower of Christ.

The more you turn from God, the more striving and confusion there will be, which results in even more fear.

You must grow in the peace of God.

When you walk in the peace of God in your home, it will crush the enemy's influence there.

If you walk in the peace of God at work, it will crush the enemy's influence there.

# Words of Wisdom

*Be very careful, then, how you live—not as unwise but as wise, making the most of every opportunity, because the days are evil. Therefore do not be foolish, but understand what the Lord's will is* (Ephesians 5:15-17 NIV).

God cannot give us happiness and peace apart from Himself, because it is not there. There is no such thing.

—C.S. Lewis, *Mere Christianity*[1]

Christ's life outwardly was one of the most troubled lives that was ever lived: tempest and tumult, tumult and tempest, the waves breaking over it all the time. But the inner life was a sea of glass. The great calm was always there.

—Henry Drummond

We must have an up-to-date, abiding relationship with Jesus to handle stress correctly. We must operate out of a heart of peace. Without this, we will be inaccurate in our discernment gift.

—Jonathan Welton, *The School of the Seers*[2]

# MY WISDOM KEYS

# 6

# *Wisdom Over Poverty*

The spirit of poverty is one of the most powerful and deadly strongholds that satan uses to keep the world in bondage. This stronghold is closely related to many fears. Most evil strongholds, which are basically deceptive patterns of thinking, are interrelated and can be overcome completely only as we unravel their entire web.

Keeping God's people oppressed and in poverty is the intent of many of the fears that the enemy of our soul sends against us. Every church and every believer must fight and overcome this spirit of poverty in order to walk in the purposes for which they are called.

[The following excerpts are adapted from *Breaking the Power of Evil*.]

# *Wisdom Over Poverty Reflections*

THE spirit of poverty is one of the enemy's most successful weapons against believers, which means that by overcoming it we gain some advances and spiritual successes. We also can gain a place of spiritual authority from which we can be used to meet some of the world's most pressing needs. Wherever this stronghold is overthrown, it is like casting off the darkness of the most terrible spiritual winter and seeing the world blossom into spring again.

The goal of the spirit of poverty is not just to keep things from us, but to keep us from the will of God. To do this, satan may even give us great riches, but our lives will be nevertheless just as empty and full of worries as if we were destitute.

Our goal for being free from the spirit of poverty is not just so we can have things that we need or want, but so that we can do the will of God without hindrance from either physical or spiritual depravity. This spirit is a yoke that manifests in both the natural and spiritual realms. Therefore, when we are freed from the yoke of the spirit of poverty, our freedom will be manifested in the natural as well as in the spiritual.

Since the Lord Jesus was completely free of the influence of this spirit, He healed the sick, raised the dead, and even multiplied food as the situation required. He always was able to draw on the resources of Heaven, which should be our goal as well.

We must settle it in our hearts and minds that as children of God He wants to make "all grace abound" to us. The goal of our faith should be to live a life of "always having all sufficiency in everything." The two key words here are *always* and *everything*. As Christians living in the Kingdom, we should always represent the life and power that are available to every citizen of the Kingdom. That does not mean that we are called to live lives that never know need. As we are told in Psalm 34:10, *"The young lions do lack and suffer hunger; but they who seek the Lord shall not be in want of any good thing."*

# *Points to Ponder*

When you overcome the spirit of poverty, you gain advances and spiritual successes.

You can also gain a place of spiritual authority from which you can be used to meet some of the world's most pressing needs.

Your goal for being free from the spirit of poverty is not just so you can have things that you need or want, but so that you can do the will of God without hindrance from either physical or spiritual depravity.

Settle in your heart and mind that as a child of God He wants to make "all grace abound" to you.

# *Words of Wisdom*

*Jesus told His disciples: "There was a rich man whose manager was accused of wasting his possessions. So he called him in and asked him, 'What is this I hear about you? Give an account of your management, because you cannot be manager any longer.' The manager said to himself, 'What shall I do now? My master is taking away my job. I'm not strong enough to dig, and I'm ashamed to beg'"* (Luke 16:1-3 NIV).

You are royalty. You can have wealth; you can have happiness, peace, joy, a long, healthy, prosperous life. These are the promises of God. But if you don't believe you can have them, you won't expect them. Because of this, you will continue to accept far less than you deserve.

—Scot Anderson, *God Wants You Rich, Not Poor & Struggling*[1]

Your vision, translated into tangible goals, will define prosperity for you, and your achievement of those goals in a manner that satisfies you means prosperity in your life. Approach the goal of defining prosperity for yourself holistically, and encompass your mental, spiritual, and physical welfare in your analysis.

—Noel Jones and Scott Chaplan, *Vow of Prosperity*[2]

Nothing is more dangerous than to be blinded by prosperity.

—John Calvin

# MY WISDOM KEYS

_____

_____

_____

_____

_____

_____

_____

_____

_____

_____

_____

_____

# 7

## *Wisdom of Learning From Mistakes*

The Church has had a long history of trying to bring the Kingdom of God to earth by might and power, without the Spirit. But the Lord stated, *"That which is born of the flesh is flesh; and that which is born of the Spirit is spirit"* (John 3:6). Even if we are trying to attain the right goal, if it is not done by the Holy Spirit, we will end up wounding instead of healing and bringing further division instead of reconciliation.

[The following excerpts are adapted from *Breaking the Power of Evil*.]

# Wisdom of Learning From Mistakes Reflections

THIS historic Church, called to carry the Gospel of salvation to the world, has been responsible for some of the deepest wounds that humankind has suffered. Inevitably the roots of these tragic mistakes can be traced to the same problem: well-intentioned people trying to use the civil realm of authority to accomplish spiritual goals. Whenever humans have tried to bring down spiritual strongholds with carnal weapons, it has resulted in a terrible defeat for the Gospel. Such actions will always lead to using another spirit to accomplish the purposes of God, and as a result the spiritual strongholds of the enemy are only made stronger, regardless of the political consequences.

The enemy knows the power of the Church when she devotes herself to the ministry of reconciliation. That is why he continually tries to divert her from this commission, and he has been very successful in doing so. Every new movement somehow allows the same seeds of its ultimate destruction to be sown within it. Churches, denominations, movements, and even individuals are still trying to conquer by might and power rather than by the Spirit—and every such "crusade" only results in more wounds.

It is true that there were many historic atrocities inflicted on Christians by Muslims and even by Jews, but that is not our problem. Regardless of what was done by others, our mistakes were the most tragic of all because they were done in the name of the Savior who had come to deliver men from such evil.

The powerful weapon of humility was demonstrated by Jesus on the cross, when He suffered the worst humiliation that the ruthless powers of this world could muster against Him for the sake of the very ones who tortured Him. In His most pressing moment, He did not ask for retaliation; He asked for forgiveness on behalf of His tormentors. By the power released through His humility, He overcame the world and was exalted to a position above all powers and authorities.

I have addressed the issues of abortion, homosexuality, and other sins of our times because the Church will never be able to be the light that can overcome this darkness until we are ourselves on the strongest foundation. When the root causes of these tragic sins are removed from the Church, we will then have the spiritual and moral authority that enables us to carry a light no darkness can overcome.

# *Points to Ponder*

The powerful weapon of humility was demonstrated by Jesus on the cross, when He suffered the worst humiliation that the ruthless powers of this world could muster against Him for the sake of the very ones who tortured Him.

In His most pressing moment, Jesus did not ask for retaliation—He asked for forgiveness on behalf of His tormentors.

By the power released through His humility, He overcame the world and was exalted to a position above all powers and authorities.

The Church will never be able to be the light that can overcome this darkness until we are on the strongest spiritual and moral foundation.

# Words of Wisdom

Sometimes zeal is less than righteous. Zeal apart from knowledge can be damning (see Rom. 10:2). Zeal without wisdom is dangerous. Zeal mixed with insensitivity is often cruel. Whenever zeal disintegrates into uncontrolled passion, it can be deadly.

—John MacArthur, *Twelve Ordinary Men*[1]

When you make a mistake, don't look back at it long. Take the reason of the thing into your mind and then look forward. Mistakes are lessons of wisdom. The past cannot be changed. The future is yet in your power.

—Hugh White

Why are we experiencing such an epidemic of open—and not-so-open—sin in the church today?... [Because] we have promoted a "gospel" that says it is possible to be a Christian while stubbornly refusing to address practices or behaviors we know are sinful. We have accepted the philosophy that it's OK for Christians to look, think, act, and talk like the world. We have made it an offense to admonish people about their sin, either privately or, when necessary, publicly. If only we were as loath to commit sin as we are to confront it!

—Nancy Leigh DeMoss, *Holiness, The Heart God Purifies*[2]

Policies are judged by their consequences, but crusades are judged by how good they make the crusaders feel.

—Thomas Sowell

# MY WISDOM KEYS

_____

_____

_____

_____

_____

_____

_____

_____

_____

_____

_____

_____

_____

_____

# 8

# *Wisdom Thwarts Evil*

If we are going to be revealed as sons and daughters of the King of kings, we must walk in a manner worthy of this high calling, which is to walk by the highest standards of integrity in all things.

Being able to discern the schemes of the enemy is the biggest part of the battle, but it is not the whole battle. We must take our stand and resist the enemy until he flees. If the attack is personal, you can do this personally. If the attack is more public, such as coming against your church, you may have to take a more public stand.

[The following excerpts are adapted from *Breaking the Power of Evil*.]

# Wisdom Thwarts Evil Reflections

Acouple of years ago a prophetic friend of mine told me of a vision he had received that concerned me and our ministry, MorningStar. He saw our ministry as a warship and I was standing on the bridge. The enemy came as a submarine and fired three torpedoes. The first torpedo was named "Friendly Fire," the next one "the Media," and the last "Witchcraft." They all struck our ship and rocked it. However, none of them did any real damage but just "shined us up" by knocking off the dead paint.

In this vision, I was so focused on looking ahead that I did not pay any attention to the attacks. This was a warning. My friend said that as the captain of the ship, I needed to deal with these attacks.

Not long after this vision, some people who had quickly become some of the best friends our ministry had ever had just as quickly turned against us. They made a number of wild and blatantly false accusations against us. I took the issue before our local congregation. I tried to do it with as much grace as possible, but I did address the issues and the false accusations directly. They stopped immediately, and what had been a big discouragement became a source of peace and confidence in our people.

Then the second torpedo hit. It was an article written in a Christian magazine about me and the ministry. After attempts to get the owner of this magazine to correct the inaccuracies and false statements about us, I then publicly answered it. Again, what was a devastating attack turned into a positive.

The last attack, from witchcraft, rose up in the most blatant form I had ever experienced in a local church setting. A large, international New Age community started putting the word out that they were going to drive us away. Again, I took a public stand, and it broke almost immediately.

There is a time to turn the other cheek to one who strikes us, and there is a time to stand up and defend ourselves. If I had taken these attacks too personally, I do not think that I could have responded rightly, and I even could have aggravated the attacks. That is one way that I have learned to distinguish the attacks that are coming as discipline from the Lord, and that I simply need to cover with love, from those that I need to respond to for the sake of those who have been entrusted to my oversight.

# *Points to Ponder*

There is a time to turn the other cheek to one who strikes you, and there is a time to stand up and defend yourself.

Are you more prone to turn the other cheek or defend yourself?

Do you ever take attacks too personally?

Can you respond rightly when you are taking things personally?

Can you distinguish the attacks that are coming as discipline from the Lord and those coming from the evil one?

# *Words of Wisdom*

Fear-driving religion is terribly evil. It manipulates people's sense of guilt and uses familial loyalties to imprison families for generations. It aims to keep people so preoccupied with religious activity that they are too busy to hear truth and too bound to accept it.

—Jeff Rostocil, *Unshakable*[1]

*Then the Lord God said, "Behold, the man has become like one of Us, knowing good and evil; and now, he might stretch out his hand, and take also from the tree of life, and eat, and live forever"* (Genesis 3:22).

Complacency is killing Christians. The attitude *it won't happen to me and mine* doesn't work. In the homes of those who bury their heads in the sand, a killer stalks to steal ideals, values, and morals, and eventually it destroys the family.

—Doug Stringer, *Hope for a Fatherless Generation*[2]

*But the Lord is faithful, and He will strengthen and protect you from the evil one* (2 Thessalonians 3:3).

# MY WISDOM KEYS

# 9

# *Wisdom Against Idols*

To worship an image of God rather than God is a serious departure from true worship, but there is a way in which many, if not most, Christians do this and are not aware of it. We can come up with our own image of God in our minds and worship it in place of God. I am not talking here about a physical representation of what we think God looks like, but our concept of who God is and what He is like that is born out of our own idealism rather than revealed truth.

[The following excerpts are adapted from *Breaking the Power of Evil*.]

# Wisdom Against Idols Reflections

HUMAN idealism is one of the greatest obstacles to truth. Human idealism is born out of the good side of the Tree of Knowledge and will have all of the appearances of being good, but its fruit is deadly. Much of the teaching and theology that is prevalent in the Church today has its source in man rather than in the Scriptures. This is what happened to the Pharisees, who were the most devoted to the Scriptures in biblical times, but they still allowed the traditions of men to eclipse the revealed truth of the Scriptures.

We not only do this with God, but we do it with men and women of God as well. Paul the apostle was probably very different from the picture that most Christians have of him, as were most of the men and women of God in Scripture—as are most men and women of God who are alive today! We can form our own image of what someone is like from their television programs, books, and tapes, or even from sitting under their preaching personally. It is not that we always make them out to be better than they really are; they may in fact be much better than we perceive them to be, but it is still our own image of them rather than who they really are. This is a form of deception.

We must admit that most Christians have built protective walls and barriers around their perceptions of the truth—and guard them furiously. This only reveals that they are, in fact, worshiping a graven image. Even if the part that they have is completely accurate and true, we all "know in part," and therefore it is at best incomplete.

The idolatry of humankind is one of the reasons that the great time of trouble is coming upon the earth in these last days. These troubles will reveal for all time just how shaky our misplaced trust in anything but God really is.

Where do we have the most invested? Where our treasure is, there will our hearts be also (see Matt. 6:21). Are our hearts more with this present world than in the Kingdom? If so, we will have all the fears that this world has. If so, we will be shaken when the earth shakes. The Lord is coming back to liberate the entire earth. For Him to do this, the entire earth must be shaken loose from its trust in idols.

# *Points to Ponder*

Have you built protective walls and barriers around your perceptions of the truth? Do you guard them furiously?

The idolatry of humankind is one of the reasons that the great time of trouble is coming upon the earth in these last days.

Troubles reveal just how shaky your misplaced trust in anything but God really is.

Where do you have the most invested?

Where your treasure is, there will your heart be also. (See Luke 12:34 KJV.)

# *Words of Wisdom*

*You shall not make for yourself an idol, or any likeness of what is in heaven above or on the earth beneath or in the water under the earth* (Deuteronomy 5:8).

O ye sons of men, think not that God is blind. He can perceive the idols in your hearts; He understands what be the secret things that your souls lust after; He searches your heart, He tries your reins; beware lest He find you sacrificing to strange gods, for His anger will smoke against you, and His jealousy will be stirred. O ye that worship not God, the God of Israel, who give Him not dominion over your whole soul, and live not to His honor, repent ye of your idolatry, seek mercy through the blood of Jesus, and provoke not the Lord to jealousy any more.

—C.H. Spurgeon[1]

When we focus solely on the Word, eventually we begin to fight amongst ourselves over the Word. We begin to pull apart the Body of Christ because there is a right and a wrong. And when the teachers disagree, and many do, there is division. Leader after leader begins to assert his or her case of doctrine and theology and builds a case to prove his or hers and disprove the others.

—Danny Silk, *Culture of Honor*[2]

A god who let us prove his existence would be an idol.

—Dietrich Bonhoeffer

# MY WISDOM KEYS

_____

_____

_____

_____

_____

_____

_____

_____

_____

_____

_____

_____

_____

# 10

# *Wisdom to Escape the Wilderness*

Complaining can be one of the most powerful enemies that keeps us from walking in His purposes for our lives.

I was told that during this time of being put in the Lord's holding pattern, we were going to be tried by depression. For someone like me to wait is one of the most depressing things there is. I know that many in our congregation have already spent years waiting on God, and just the mention of having to wait longer will be understandably difficult. Even so, if we give in to depression or doubt, it will cause us to stay in the wilderness even longer.

[The following excerpts are adapted from *High Calling*.]

# Wisdom to Escape the Wilderness Reflections

**D**EPRESSION is sin because whatever is not of faith is sin, and depression does not embrace faith. It takes faith to inherit the promises of God.

Some chemical and biological problems can cause depression, but most of the depression that we suffer has a spiritual root. A victory over every spiritual stronghold was gained for us at the cross. We must not be satisfied with anything less than a complete victory over depression, and determine that we are going to view every situation with faith, not doubt. If we are getting tired of the wilderness, it is time to review the promises of God, and encourage ourselves in His faithfulness.

Depression basically comes from seeing our situation from the dark side. This happens whenever we stop looking through the eyes of faith. Depression caused ten of the twelve spies who were sent to look over the Promised Land to come back with an *"evil report"* (Num. 13:32 KJV). It is interesting that their report of the land was true, and was basically the same report given by the two faithful spies, Joshua and Caleb. However, the ten saw the obstacles as being too great for them to overcome, while Joshua and Caleb believed they could be overcome since God was on their side. In both cases, it was not what they saw that differed, but how they saw it.

Like the first generation of Israel to come out of Egypt, many Christians never walk in the promises of God to which they are called because they fall into grumbling and complaining. Sadly, many succumb to this just before they are about to be released from the wilderness. Having been there so long, the temptation to doubt is the greatest then.

The fastest way out of the wilderness is to be thankful, even for the wilderness. We enter the Lord's gates *"with thanksgiving, and His courts with praise"* (Ps. 100:4). Let's determine that we are going to abide in Him in every area of our lives, and we can do this by being thankful for everything.

Let's war against any tendency to complain about anyone or anything, but rather in all things give thanks. Let's enter His gates with thanksgiving and His courts with praise—and stay there.

# Points to Ponder

If you are getting tired of the wilderness, it is time to review the promises of God, and encourage yourself in His faithfulness.

Depression basically comes from seeing your situation from the dark side—don't stop looking through the eyes of faith.

Are you walking in your calling—or grumbling and complaining?

The fastest way out of the wilderness is to be thankful, even for the wilderness.

Determine to abide in Him in every area of your life by being thankful for everything.

# Words of Wisdom

Your dream is powerful. Draw on that power to help you stay focused and lock fear out of your life. When you force your fear to look your dream in the eye, fear doesn't stand a chance of winning.

—Mark J. Chironna, *Live Your Dream*[1]

*Whatever is true, whatever is honorable, whatever is right, whatever is pure, whatever is lovely, whatever is of good repute, if there is any excellence and if anything worthy of praise, dwell on these things* (Philippians 4:8).

*The dark night of the soul.* This phenomenon describes a malady that the greatest of Christians have suffered from time to time. It was the malady that provoked David to soak his pillow with tears. It was the malady that earned for Jeremiah the sobriquet, "The Weeping Prophet." It was the malady that so afflicted Martin Luther that his melancholy threatened to destroy him. This is no ordinary fit of depression, but it is a depression that is linked to a crisis of faith, a crisis that comes when one senses the absence of God or gives rise to a feeling of abandonment by Him.

—R.C. Sproul, *The Dark Night of the Soul*[2]

The wilderness is a place of dying, where all the things that cause you to stumble in your walk with God are killed.

—T.D. Jakes, *Wisdom From T.D. Jakes*[3]

# My Wisdom Keys

_____

_____

_____

_____

_____

_____

_____

_____

_____

_____

_____

_____

_____

_____

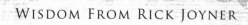
_____

_____

_____

_____

_____

_____

_____

_____

_____

_____

_____

_____

_____

_____

_____

_____

_____

_____

_____

_____

_____

_____

_____

# 11

## *Wisdom of Fear*

The fear of the Lord is required if we are to receive His guidance and instruction or receive our inheritance. The goal of truth is not just so we can know the way, but also so that we will walk in the way. Without a solid foundation of the pure and holy fear of the Lord, we will build our lives on the weak foundation of knowing the truth but not doing it. Therefore, the true nature of our spiritual lives is revealed in the way we behave when no one is looking and when we know no one could find out. Who we are in secret before God is who we are.

[The following excerpts are adapted from *High Calling*.]

# Wisdom of Fear Reflections

THE one who fears the Lord and receives His instruction will abide in prosperity and His children will inherit the land. This is the foundation of the true nobility. The original purpose of the nobility was to plant righteous families in the earth who would be righteous generation after generation. These were also the land owners, because the righteous were to inherit the land. Of course, this was perverted whenever a generation did not walk in the fear of the Lord.

However, to plant a family in the earth who walks in the fear of the Lord is still our calling and should be the goal of every Christian. As we walk in the fear of the Lord, and pass this on to our children, our families will prosper, inherit the land, and be righteous seeds in the earth.

As we are told in Proverbs 22:1, *"A good name is to be more desired than great wealth, favor is better than silver and gold."* Those who fear the Lord determine that they will establish a name that is esteemed for truth, honor, integrity, and true Christian charity. We must impart to our children the knowledge that the true fear of the Lord is our most valuable possession, and that to live our lives to serve and obey Him is the highest calling. Those who walk in this are the true nobility. Their names are not just known on the earth; they are written in the Book of Life.

The first Adam had a bride who lived in a perfect world, yet chose to sin. The "last Adam," Jesus, will have a Bride who lives in a most imperfect world, but chooses to obey. This is our calling and is a success whose treasure will last forever.

# Points to Ponder

If you fear the Lord and receive His instruction, you will abide in prosperity and His children will inherit the land.

The original purpose of the nobility was to plant righteous families in the earth who would be righteous generation after generation.

If you fear the Lord, you will establish a name that is esteemed for truth, honor, integrity, and true Christian charity.

Impart to your children the knowledge that the true fear of the Lord is their most valuable possession, and that to live their lives to serve and obey Him is their highest calling.

# Words of Wisdom

*So the church throughout all Judea and Galilee and Samaria enjoyed peace, being built up; and going on in the fear of the Lord and in the comfort of the Holy Spirit, it continued to increase* (Acts 9:31).

The fear of the Lord tends to take away all other fears... This is the secret of Christian courage and boldness.

—Sinclair B. Ferguson, *Grow in Grace*[1]

I have never once feared the devil, but I tremble every time I enter the pulpit.

—John Knox

*The fear of the Lord is the beginning of knowledge; fools despise wisdom and instruction* (Proverbs 1:7).

# MY WISDOM KEYS

# 12

## *Wisdom to Change*

Sociologists have long been baffled at the extraordinary resistance many people have toward change. They are still hard pressed to explain why the child of alcoholic parents will so often marry a heavy drinker, knowing all of the pain and turmoil that can be expected. However, the fear of change is often stronger than the fear of such pain and turmoil.

[The following excerpts are adapted from *High Calling*.]

# Wisdom to Change Reflections

THIS fear of change is popularly referred to as "the tyranny of the familiar." It is precisely what turns Christians into "old wineskins." New wine is still expanding, and an old wineskin is one that is too rigid and inflexible to hold new wine.

It is comforting to know that the Lord never changes. However, if we are going to be like Him, most of us still have a lot of changing to do! Until we are like Him and doing the works that He did, we are not finished with the process yet. Therefore, we can expect a lifetime of changing. One of the ways that the Lord keeps us flexible is to "pour us into a new vessel" whenever we start becoming too comfortable and resistant to change. We may think that the shocking changes that come into our lives are the result of the devil's attack, but even if they are, the Lord had to allow them, so we can assume that we need them. Many of these changes are possibly even in answer to our prayers not to become old wineskins.

If we remain open to the changes He wants to bring, including the new things He is doing that we may not understand yet, we probably will not have to endure nearly the amount of shaking that we otherwise would. If we are wise, we will learn to embrace change as the great opportunity for spiritual growth that it is. Usually when we are resistant to change it is because we are placing our security in our environment instead of in the Lord.

I do not think that I know a single Christian who has not been through some kind of traumatic church problem or split. Even so, the wise do not base their vision or theology on the mistakes of the past, but learn the necessary lessons, allowing the experience to purify them so that they have a more clear vision for the future. We must continue to move forward. Every time the wine is poured into a new vessel, there is a great deal of commotion, but the purity is worth it.

# *Points to Ponder*

It is comforting to know that the Lord never changes.

If you are going to be like Him, you may still have a lot of changing to do.

You can expect a lifetime of changing.

One of the ways that the Lord keeps you flexible is to pour you into a new vessel whenever you become too comfortable and resistant to change.

If you are wise, you will learn to embrace change as the great opportunity for spiritual growth that it is.

# *Words of Wisdom*

It is true that Jesus calls us friends, but you must have discernment and wisdom to understand what He means in this context. You see, it's one thing for Jesus to call you His friend, but it's another thing for you to be a friend to Him.

—David E. Taylor, *Face-to-Face Appearances From Jesus*[1]

*In a moment, in the twinkling of an eye, at the last trumpet; for the trumpet will sound, and the dead will be raised imperishable, and we will be changed* (1 Corinthians 15:52).

For too many years, Christians did not even realize that demons existed, and therefore did not guard against them. They are such evil creatures, and they are always looking for a body to enter.

—Delores Winder, *Surprised by Healing*[2]

Everybody is in favor of progress. It's the change they don't like.

—Author Unknown

# MY WISDOM KEYS

# 13

## Wisdom of God's Heart

If we knew that we had less than 24 hours to live, our prayers would probably be the most focused that they have ever been on the deepest issues of our hearts. We can, therefore, consider the prayer that Jesus prayed on the night He was betrayed to be just that—the revelation of the deepest concerns of His heart. Therefore, John 17 may be the most pure reflection of the heart of God. Obviously, one of the deepest issues of His heart was the unity of His people.

[The following excerpts are adapted from *High Calling*.]

# Wisdom of God's Heart Reflections

ONE of the basic characteristics of God is unity. The Father, Son, and Holy Spirit are always in perfect unity. There is never any jealousy, contention, strife, or discord in the Trinity. The closer we become to being changed into the image of the Lord, the more unity we will have with Him and one another. It is by beholding His glory that this will be accomplished. He gave us His glory that we might be one, and to the degree that we have beheld His glory, we will have unity.

The reverse is also true. If there is discord in the Church, it is because we have taken our eyes off the Lord and are no longer beholding His glory. Knowing that one of the deepest desires of the Lord's heart is the unity of His people, how could anyone who truly loves the Savior willfully bring discord to the Church that He died to save and unify?

Bitterness, wrath, anger, clamor, and slander grieve the Holy Spirit because they destroy the unity of His people. Therefore, we should always endeavor to obey the exhortation here by not letting any unwholesome word proceed from our mouth, but only those that bring edification to His people.

As a parent, there are few things that bless me more than seeing my children loving and getting along with each other. Likewise, there are few things that bring me more grief than when they begin to fight or get angry with each other. Remember, the unity of His people is one of the deepest issues of God's heart.

If we love Him, should we not utterly devote ourselves to that which is so obviously important to Him?

The Scriptures are clear that the Church will attain unity before the end comes. The Lord's Prayer will be answered, and we will be perfected in unity. Let us all determine that we will be part of helping this come to pass, and not be a stumbling block to it.

# *Points to Ponder*

If there is discord, it is because you have taken your eyes off the Lord and are no longer beholding His glory.

Knowing that one of the deepest desires of the Lord's heart is the unity of His people, can you willfully bring discord to the Church that He died to save and unify?

Say only those things that bring edification to His people.

The unity of His people is one of the deepest issues of God's heart. If you love Him, devote yourself to that which is so obviously important to Him.

# Words of Wisdom

*Behold, how good and how pleasant it is for brothers to dwell together in unity!* (Psalm 133:1)

Has it ever occurred to you that one hundred pianos all tuned to the same fork are automatically tuned to each other? They are of one accord by being tuned, not to each other, but to another standard to which each one must individually bow. So one hundred worshipers [meeting] together, each one looking away to Christ, are in heart nearer to each other than they could possibly be, were they to become "unity" conscious and turn their eyes away from God to strive for closer fellowship. Social religion is perfected when private religion is purified.

—A.W. Tozer, *The Pursuit of God*

There is no hero in the Bible who is exempt from the truth—even David, to whom God refers as *"a man after His own heart"* (1 Sam. 13:14). David's relationship with Bathsheba began as a rooftop affair and unfolds in a three-act play of crime, cover-up, and confession.

—Ruth and Elmer Towns, *How to Build a Lasting Marriage*[1]

95

# MY WISDOM KEYS

_____

_____

_____

_____

_____

_____

_____

_____

_____

_____

_____

_____

_____

_____

# 14

## Wisdom and Truth

One of the primary ways that we grow up into Christ is by *"speaking the truth in love"* (Eph. 4:15). Jesus is the Truth, and if we are going to abide in Him, we must be committed to truth. God is also love, so if we are going to be like Him, we must do all that we do in love.

[The following excerpts are adapted from *High Calling*.]

# Wisdom and Truth Reflections

ONE of the basic characteristics of God is that His Word is true! How can we ever expect to abide in Him, be like Him, or represent Him, if we are not devoted to truth? The devil is the father of lies, and when we have given ourselves to lying, in any form or to any degree, we are opening ourselves up to the devil, to be used by him, and to be changed into his image instead of Christ's.

It should be a basic goal of every Christian to walk in truth and love in everything that we do and say. If we do not, we will remain the hypocrites that the world thinks we are. We should also keep in mind that the Lord Himself reserved His most scathing denunciations for the religious hypocrites.

We should examine every conflict that we are now involved in to be sure that we are walking in both truth and love in it. Is our position truly accurate, or have we let partial truths, or even lies get in? Once our argument or position in a conflict passes the truth test, we should then determine that it also passes the love test. Then we should endeavor to test all our words and actions this way.

This means that sometimes we will not say things that may be true unless we can also say them in love. Truth can hurt, and even kill, if it is not spoken in the right spirit. That is why *"Satan disguises himself as an angel of light"* (see 2 Cor. 11:14). This could also be translated "messenger of truth." Many of the devil's most devastating attacks will have some basis in truth.

Often it will have a twisted interpretation, or be used to gain entry for his subsequent lies, but sometimes it is just plain truth that is incomplete, or spoken in bad timing so that its effect is to cause division, discord, and so on. That is why we must also determine if we are speaking the truth *"in love."* Satan can use truth as a weapon for evil, but he has a very hard time masquerading love.

# Points to Ponder

Can you abide in Him, be like Him, or represent Him,
if you are not devoted to truth?

Your goal should be to walk in truth and love in everything
that you do and say.

You should also keep in mind that the Lord Himself
reserved His most scathing denunciations for the
religious hypocrites.

Examine every conflict that you are now involved in to be
sure that you are walking in both truth and love.

Is your position truly accurate, or have you allowed partial
truths or even lies to get in?

# Words of Wisdom

Apparently the Holy Spirit had hit a vein of truth and had uncovered the real problem. It was not what they had thought, but the Holy Spirit had revealed to them the real issue they were facing.

—Larry Kreider and Dennis De Grasse,
*Supernatural Living*[1]

The search for truth then becomes all-pervasive, drawing implications for the essence and destiny of life itself. Even if not overtly admitted, the search for truth is nevertheless hauntingly present, propelled by the need for incontrovertible answers to four inescapable questions, those dealing with origin, meaning, morality, and destiny —connecting the what with the why. No thinking person can avoid this search, and it can only end when one is convinced that the answers espoused are true. Aristotle was right when he said that all philosophy begins with wonder; but the journey, I suggest, can only progress with truth.

—Ravi Zacharias, *This We Believe*[2]

One never errs more safely than when one errs by too much loving the truth.

—Augustine

*So Jesus was saying to those Jews who had believed Him, "If you continue in My word, then you are truly disciples of Mine; and you will know the truth, and the truth will make you free"* (John 8:31-32).

## MY WISDOM KEYS

_____

_____

_____

_____

_____

_____

_____

_____

_____

_____

_____

_____

_____

_____

# 15

## *Wisdom Versus Idealism*

Second only to the theologies and beliefs developed by wounds, rejection, and failures, idealism is one of the most effective enemies of the truth. This deception is usually rooted more in a lack of experience and the wisdom that comes from that experience.

Idealism has also proven especially deadly because it is usually rooted in a sincere religious zeal. After all, it is difficult for the devil to stop people who are in pursuit of the truth, yet he knows that he can often accomplish even more destruction by getting behind them and pushing them too far.

[The following excerpts are adapted from *Delivered From Evil*.]

# Wisdom Versus Idealism Reflections

RELIGIOUS idealism is the tendency to take things beyond what the Lord has directed.

The problem here is not religious zeal. After all, zeal is something that most believers can use in greater measure. The problem comes when Christians combine this zeal with pride, which results in idealism, and therefore becomes destructive. It is especially deceptive because it has such an appearance of goodness and zeal. However, it is goodness from the Tree of the Knowledge of Good and Evil, and therefore has a deadly fruit.

Have you ever wondered why so many of the seemingly most effective teachers, counselors, and authors who speak about what a glorious Christian marriage is supposed to be like end up in divorce themselves? Just as human idealism has been one of the greatest enemies of the emerging of the glorious Church, human idealism can also be found at the root of the most destructive forces tearing apart marriages and families.

I have known many with great marriages, but I have never known anyone with a perfect marriage. I have witnessed many who would probably at least have a good marriage, and maybe even a great one, who are instead divorced because of the discouragement and frustration created by unrealistic ideals and expectations sown in them.

The Lord wants every husband to love his wife just as Christ loves the Church. Without question the Lord loves His Bride more than we can humanly perceive, or have the capacity to love ourselves. He is therefore not calling men to love their wives as much as He loves His Church, but in the same way. He laid down His life for His Bride, and we are called to lay down our lives for our wives as well. However, the modern, human ideals of this love and the way that the Lord loves His Church are often very different.

For example, have you ever considered the persecution, attacks by the devil, and other problems that the Lord allows His Bride to suffer? It is sometimes hard to understand this kind of love, but it is a higher love, and one that human idealism cannot understand.

# *Points to Ponder*

Have you ever wondered why so many of the seemingly most effective teachers, counselors, and authors who speak about what a glorious Christian marriage is supposed to be like end up in divorce themselves?

Human idealism has been one of the greatest enemies of the emerging of the glorious Church.

Many divorces occur because of the discouragement and frustration created by unrealistic ideals and expectations sown in them.

The Lord wants every husband to love his wife just as Christ loves the Church.

# Words of Wisdom

What is in your alabaster box? Is your box full of fantasies that began as a little girl while you listened to and watched fairy tales about an enchanting couple living happily ever after?

—Jackie Kendall and Debby Jones,
*Lady in Waiting*[1]

Our creation as sexual beings, especially as it is played out in the intimacy of the act of marriage, tells the story of a higher reality in a symbolic and poetic way.

—Angus N. Hunter,
*From Venus to Mars and Back*[2]

No one parents effectively by accident. Effective parenting must be intentional; it must be planned, focused, and have an expected end in mind.

—Myles Munroe and David Burrows,
*Kingdom Parenting*[3]

*For the word of God is living and active and sharper than any two-edged sword, and piercing as far as the division of soul and spirit, of both joints and marrow, and able to judge the thoughts and intentions of the heart* (Hebrews 4:12).

# MY WISDOM KEYS

_____

_____

_____

_____

_____

_____

_____

_____

_____

_____

_____

_____

# 16

# *Wisdom Beyond Human Ability*

I have come to believe that all human responsibilities are beyond human ability. This means that there is nothing we can do right without God. Because I cannot micro-manage our ministry, there is plenty of room for Him to move and for others to grow in the ministry. This is not to promote irresponsibility on my part, such as not spending the right amount of time with the ministry or with my family, but the right amount is found in each of these areas by following the Lord and being obedient day by day. I will not get anything right if I do not get this part right.

[The following excerpts are adapted from *High Calling*.]

# Wisdom Beyond Human Ability Reflections

**S**TUDIES have shown that one minute of rage can sap the strength of a normal eight-hour period. Just being angry for a few minutes can do the same thing. Worry also drains our energy at an amazing rate, even much faster than hard labor. How much more effective could we be, and how much more energy would we have, if we would abide in the peace of the Lord? Could this be why Paul wrote that *"the God of peace will soon crush Satan under your feet"* (Rom. 16:20)?

This is also a reason why elders in the church cannot be *"quick-tempered"* (Titus 1:7), or given to outbursts of anger. There are few things that can sap our effectiveness like anger or fear. In contrast, faith releases the power that created the universe.

We often think of great faith as something that happens spontaneously so that we can be used for a miracle or healing. However, the greatest faith of all, and the most effective, is to live day by day trusting Him. Then we can look at every problem as an opportunity to see His work in our lives. It is not worrying, but rather trusting and abiding in the peace of God that will crush anything that satan tries to do to us. If the Lord created the world out of chaos, He can easily deal with any problem that we have.

I have heard many Christians say that they know the Lord can do miracles, but they just do not know if He will. However, He has said that He always will do miracles if we believe Him.

We have been promised that we are entering a time when we will see great miracles. We need to also understand that this is probably because we are being thrust into a place where we are going to need them. Even so, this is what most of us have signed up for. We want to be part of what God is building, not what humans are building.

Let us determine to abide in the peace of God so that we can see the God of peace crush satan under our feet. We must also recognize anger and wrath as the great enemies of our purposes. We cannot allow them to gain entry into the fortress of faith that we are called to build.

# *Points to Ponder*

All human responsibilities are beyond human ability. This means that there is nothing you can do right without God.

One minute of rage can sap the strength of a normal eight-hour period.

Worry drains your energy at an amazing rate, even faster than hard labor.

How much more effective could you be, and how much more energy would you have, if you would abide in the peace of the Lord?

Recognize anger and wrath as the great enemies of your purpose. Don't allow them to gain entry into your fortress of faith.

# Words of Wisdom

*And looking at them Jesus said to them, "With people this is impossible, but with God all things are possible"* (Matthew 19:26).

God speaks to us and brings us revelation knowledge. Not only does He impart the word of God, but He puts His own God-breathed ideas into our minds. His ideas are always ones of success.

—Frank Bailey, *Holy Spirit, the Promised One*[1]

Yet the duties God requires of us are not in proportion to the strength we possess in ourselves. Rather, they are proportional to the resources available to us in Christ. We do not have the ability in ourselves to accomplish the least of God's tasks. This is a law of grace. When we recognize it is impossible to perform a duty in our own strength, we will discover the secret of its accomplishment. But alas, this is a secret we often fail to discover.

—John Owen, *Sin and Temptation*[2]

One great paradox of the Christian life is that we are fully responsible for our Christian growth and at the same time fully dependent upon the Holy Spirit to give us both the desire to grow and the ability to do it. God's grace does not negate the need for responsible action on our part, but rather makes it possible.

—Jerry Bridges, *Transforming Grace*[3]

# MY WISDOM KEYS

_____

_____

_____

_____

_____

_____

_____

_____

_____

_____

_____

_____

_____

# 17

# *Wisdom and Miracles*

Many want to see miracles, but how many are willing to be put in a place where they need one? Miracles are not given for our entertainment; neither are they given to build our faith. They are the result of *having* faith. Almost every miracle was the result of a desperate need. The greater the need, the greater the miracle.

[The following excerpts are adapted from *High Calling.*]

# Wisdom and Miracles Reflections

**H**OW great would the miracle have been to feed the five thousand if the disciples had hundreds of fish and loaves, and just needed a few more? It was a great miracle because they had so little in their own hands with which to fulfill God's command.

When we are called by God to do a task, we often begin to look at what resources we have to perform it. This can be the beginning of our fall from the faith that will be required to do the true works of God. It is at the point that we see our resources running out that we will experience the power of God. What we need to do the true works of God will not be found in our own resources, or our own wisdom, but in the limitless resources of God.

We will never be adequate within ourselves for what the Lord calls us to do. In our flesh, which is our natural strength, we cannot accomplish one thing for the Lord. That is why the apostle Paul told the men of Athens that the Lord is not *"served by human hands"* (see Acts 17:24-25). Only the Spirit can beget that which is spirit. We are utterly dependent on the Lord to do His work. We will never be adequate within ourselves for His work, and if we ever start to feel adequate, we will almost certainly be in the midst of a fall from grace.

True faith is not a feeling of adequacy in ourselves, but a steady focus on the adequacy of God. True faith is not a faith in our faith, but a faith in Him. The greatest faith is that which can see and believe in His provision in the time of the most pressing need. We need to see every circumstance that is beyond ourselves as an opportunity to see a miracle. If we are faithful in the little opportunities, He will bless us with greater ones. And yes, those blessings are trials.

We are about to see great miracles, because He is going to allow us to come into places where we are going to need them. Prepare for these opportunities by focusing on Him today.

# *Points to Ponder*

Miracles are not given for your entertainment; neither are they given to build your faith. They are the result of *having* faith.

When you are called by God to do a task, do you often begin to look at what resources you have to perform it?

What you need to do the true works of God will not be found in your own resources, or your own wisdom, but in the limitless resources of God.

You will never be adequate within yourself for what the Lord calls you to do.

The greatest faith is that which can see and believe in His provision in the time of the most pressing need.

# *Words of Wisdom*

Before I was saved, I called myself a scientific atheist. My wife and I had not been churchgoers, but on the day we were saved, we began to read the Bible and decided simply to believe it. From the first day of our new life in Christ, miracles began to happen.

—Alan Vincent, *The Good Fight of Faith*[1]

I confessed my helplessness to change, and the Lord met me with compassion and forgiveness. The Lord never points a finger to condemn us. Condemnation and accusation come from the devil.

—Sid Roth, *Supernatural Healing*[2]

Immediately the woman fell to the ground, crying hysterically. The man continued to prophesy things like, "The sun is yellow. The moon is yellow." When the woman finally regained her composure, she explained, "I have a son who is autistic and I told the Lord today, 'If You are going to heal my son, have someone tell me that I have on a yellow shirt.'"

—Kris Vallotton, *Developing a Supernatural Lifestyle*[3]

A miracle is an extraordinary event wrought by God through human agency, an event that cannot be explained by natural forces. Miracles are always designed to authenticate the human instrument. God has chosen to declare a specific revelation to those who witness the miracle.

—John MacArthur, *Charismatic Chaos*[4]

# MY WISDOM KEYS

_____

_____

_____

_____

_____

_____

_____

_____

_____

_____

_____

_____

_____

_____

# 18

## Wisdom of Democracy

Because I have something of a prophetic reputation, I am continually asked my opinion about current events. This is a serious problem because I can give my opinion, and it is often related as being a prophecy even when I make it clear that it is an opinion and not a prophecy. I do not presume to know the Lord's perspective on everything or even many things that relate to current events. I used to take His silence as rejection, but now I feel that there may be a message in it.

[The following excerpts are adapted from *High Calling*.]

# *Wisdom of Democracy Reflections*

THE last time God would not speak to me on a matter that I earnestly sought Him about was the Y2K matter. For months I inquired of Him, with no response. Finally, when He did speak to me about it, He merely said that He was not speaking about it because it was not going to be anything of consequence. That, of course, turned out to be exactly right.

I have learned that many things in my personal life that I can be consumed with usually turn out to be insignificant, and therefore just a waste of my worries. I have also learned that many things that capture the interest and concern of the world do not even cause a ripple in Heaven. Usually it is for the same reason; these matters turn out to be unimportant. Because of this, I try to pray every day to see with His eyes, hear with His ears, and understand with His heart. I do not claim to be anywhere close to this now, but I believe that this is the calling of every Christian, not just those who are called prophetically.

I also like to watch the news and follow politics and business because they can reveal the heart of the people who we are called to reach. However, it is crucial that we are able to separate what the people are saying from what God is saying. These two are often not only different but in opposition to each other. Even so, we can be thankful for democracy, as it is obviously the best form of government on earth. We can have the most perfect form of government, but it will be no better than the men and women who are in it.

The United States is not the Kingdom of God and will have its flaws until the King returns. Perfect justice is humanly impossible. It is time we realize that we have always been in that place where perfect justice and perfect government are not humanly possible. Even so, because I have traveled much of the world and have seen alternative governments with all their flaws, I am profoundly thankful to be an American and to live in a democracy.

# Points to Ponder

Have you learned that many things in your personal life usually turn out to be insignificant, and a waste of your worries?

Do you realize that many things capturing the interest and concern of the world do not even cause a ripple in Heaven?

Pray every day to see with His eyes, hear with His ears, and understand with His heart.

This is the calling of every Christian, not just those who are called prophetically.

It is crucial that you separate what the people are saying from what God is saying. These two are often not only different but in opposition to each other.

# Words of Wisdom

Why do authorities exist? It is because we live in a sinful and fallen world, and without authority everyone would do "what is right in his own eyes," resulting in chaos. Those who will not be constrained from within by the living presence of Jesus Christ, must be restrained from without by the state, acting under God's ultimate authority, in order to "promote the general welfare," in the words of the Constitution's preamble.

—Cal Thomas, *"The Authority of the State"*[1]

*He loves righteousness and justice; the earth is full of the lovingkindness of the Lord* (Psalm 33:5).

Can we pray for justice, and yet love our enemy at the same time? The answer is yes...We will magnify the mercy of God by praying for our enemies to be saved and reconciled to God. At the personal level we will be willing to suffer for their everlasting good, and we will give them food and drink. We will put away malicious hatred and private vengeance. But at the public level we will also magnify the justice of God by praying and working for justice to be done on earth, if necessary through wise and measured force from God-ordained authority.

—John Piper[2]

Justice denied anywhere diminishes justice everywhere.

—Martin Luther King Jr.

# MY WISDOM KEYS

_____

_____

_____

_____

_____

_____

_____

_____

_____

_____

_____

_____

_____

_____

# 19

# *Wisdom to Destroy Racism*

Racism is one of the ultimate strongholds that binds humankind, and it is the primary stronghold that empowers the spirit of death. It is the linchpin yoke of bondage that empowers satan's cord of three strands. For this reason, he seeks to impose it on every church and movement that is making a spiritual advance. It has been an effective strategy since most in history have fallen to this great evil in at least one of its forms. Because deception is deceptive, those who are bound by it often believe they are the most free from the prejudices of racism.

[The following excerpts are adapted from *Overcoming Evil in the Last Days*.]

# Wisdom to Destroy Racism Reflections

E must understand how racism is rooted in two of the most basic evil powers that have controlled humankind since the Fall—fear and pride. A person becomes a racist either because of pride in the flesh or because of fear of those who are different, both of which are a thick veil over the human soul. Racism is one of the most powerful of the evil world rulers.

The harvest will come at the end of the age and will be the reaping of everything that has been sown in man, both the good and the evil. Fear and pride will come to full maturity in man at the end. When Jesus was asked about the signs that would accompany the end of the age, He said, *"Nation will rise against nation, and kingdom against kingdom..."* (Matt. 24:7).

The world is losing control of its racial problems. The cause is a spiritual power that no legislation or human agency can stop. Only that which is bound in Heaven can be bound on the earth (see Matt. 16:19). If the Church does not face this problem—overcoming the racism within our own ranks so that we can take spiritual authority over it—the world will soon fall into an abyss of chaos, destruction, and suffering of unprecedented proportions—all because of racial conflict.

What happened in Rwanda in 1994—nearly one million people were murdered—was one of satan's dress rehearsals for what he wants to release on the earth. If we are arrogant enough to believe that we live in a country too civilized for such a thing to happen, that very pride could be the only door that the devil needs. Of all the nations in Africa, Rwanda was the one where such a thing was least expected. Ninety percent Christian, the Rwandans were considered the most peaceful, loving people in Africa. Nazi Germany was also considered a Christian nation. How did the devil take them over? This is a question we must answer.

The most deadly wars in history, including World War II, were ignited by racism. This powerful spirit prepares the way for and empowers the spirit of death. The apostle Paul understood that, when the ultimate racial barrier, the division between Jew and Gentile, is overcome and they are grafted together in Christ, it will mean nothing less than *life from the dead* (Rom. 11:15), or the overcoming of death.

# *Points to Ponder*

Racism is one of the ultimate strongholds that binds humankind, and it is the primary stronghold that empowers the spirit of death.

The world is losing control of its racial problems.

No legislation or human agency can stop racism—only that which is bound in Heaven can be bound on the earth (see Matt. 16:19).

If the Church does not face this problem, the world will fall into chaos, destruction, and suffering of unprecedented proportions—all because of racial conflict.

When the division between Jew and Gentile is overcome and they are grafted together in Christ, it will mean the overcoming of death.

# Words of Wisdom

Racism isn't a bad habit; it's not a mistake; it's a sin. The answer is not sociology; it's theology.

—Tony Evans

The family of God is ethnically and culturally diverse. As Christians we not only permit such diversity, but we *cherish* it. This is because God Himself cherishes ethnic diversity. He is not *color*-blind; He is *colorful.* At His throne God welcomes worshipers *"from every nation, tribe, people and language"* (Rev. 7:9 NIV). His plan of redemption is for the peoples of the world in all their rich variety.

—Philip Graham Ryken, *Is Jesus the Only Way?[1]*

*A new commandment I give to you, that you love one another, even as I have loved you, that you also love one another* (John 13:34).

I'm planning to be civil toward any of my neighbors who may be heading for the local mosque. But in no way will I accept the charge that to tell them of the truth of the gospel of Jesus is to jeopardize the "pluralism" that has made America a great springboard of freedom for so many generations. And no way either will I concede the right—a right that has now become a duty—to tell them that the error of their thinking is profound. I will do that not because I hate them, but because I love them.

—Joel Belz[2]

# MY WISDOM KEYS

_____

_____

_____

_____

_____

_____

_____

_____

_____

_____

_____

_____

_____

_____

# 20

# *Wisdom and Love*

Loving God is the greatest commandment and the greatest gift that we can receive. The second greatest commandment is to love our neighbors. As the Lord affirmed, the whole law is fulfilled by keeping these two commandments, which means that, if we keep these two commandments, we will keep the whole law (see Matt. 22:34-40; Rom. 13:8). If we love the Lord, we will not worship idols. If we love our neighbors, we will not envy them, steal from them, murder them, and so forth. Therefore, keeping these two positive commandments to love will enable us to obey all of the negative "do not's" of the law.

[The following excerpts are adapted from *Overcoming Evil in the Last Days*.]

# Wisdom and Love Reflections

SIMPLE love for God will overcome most of the evil in our hearts, and it is the most powerful weapon against evil in the world. Because loving God is our highest goal, it must be the primary focus of our lives. To divert us from this ultimate quest, the enemy uses one of his most deceptive and deadly attacks on the Church through the religious spirit. The devil wants to keep us focused on the evil in our lives, knowing that we will become what we are beholding (see 2 Cor. 3:18). As long as we keep looking at the evil, it will continue to have dominion over us. On the contrary, when we look to the Lord and behold His glory, we will be changed into His image.

This is not to imply that we should ignore the sins and errors that are in our lives. In fact, the Scriptures command us to examine ourselves and test ourselves to be sure that we are still in the faith (see 2 Cor. 13:5). The issue is what we do after the iniquity is discovered. Do we turn to the Tree of the Knowledge of Good and Evil or to the Tree of Life? Do we try to make ourselves better so that we will then be acceptable to God, or do we turn to the cross of Jesus to find both forgiveness and power to overcome the sin?

Love opens us up to seeing much more than we could otherwise see. Love is the foundation of all true vision and true prophecy. Anything but love will distort our vision. One of the tragic mistakes genuine prophetic people make is thinking that their little part is the whole vision. Thankfully, love opens our hearts to understand others and, therefore, receive from their perspective.

Because love covers a multitude of sins, let us determine that we are going to grow in love by covering other people's sins against us. Start with the person who irritates you the most, whether it is your spouse, boss, pastor, etc. Now consider what it is they do that irritates you the most. This is your greatest opportunity to grow in love. Determine that you are going to cover that which irritates you and start praying for the Lord to bless that person. Then start using other things that irritate you as a call to grow in love. If you do this, your life will radically change and so will the lives of all who are close to you.

# *Points to Ponder*

Loving God is the greatest commandment and the greatest gift that you can receive.

The second greatest commandment is to love your neighbors.

As the Lord affirmed, the whole law is fulfilled by keeping these two commandments, which means that, if you keep these two commandments, you will keep the whole law.

Because loving God is your highest goal, it must be the primary focus of your life.

Because love covers a multitude of sins, determine to grow in love by covering other people's sins against you.

# Words of Wisdom

The engine that propels you to your place of authority is fueled by love. It is God's love that empowers you, and the fuel line of that love is God's Word.

—Faisal Malick, *Positioned to Bless*[1]

More specifically, it is abnormal for Christians not to be passionately in love with God and, in turn, enamored with the things of God. In fact, passionate love should be the substance that primarily characterizes us as believers.

—Banning Liebscher, *Jesus Culture*[2]

Real Christians do not first see that God loves them, and later on find out that He is lovely. They first see that God is lovely, that Christ is excellent and glorious. Their hearts are captivated by this view of God, and their love for God arises chiefly from this view. True love begins with God and loves Him for His own sake. Self-love begins with self, and loves God in the interests of self.

—Jonathan Edwards

*There is no fear in love; but perfect love casts out fear, because fear involves punishment, and the one who fears is not perfected in love. We love, because He first loved us. If someone says, "I love God," and hates his brother, he is a liar; for the one who does not love his brother whom he has seen, cannot love God whom he has not seen* (1 John 4:18-20).

# MY WISDOM KEYS

_____

_____

_____

_____

_____

_____

_____

_____

_____

_____

_____

_____

_____

_____

_____

# 21

## *Wisdom Over Witchcraft*

Witchcraft is basically the practice of cursing others. This cursing does not just come through cults or black magic arts; it can come through those who love us and have good intentions but are trying to manipulate us. Using manipulation or a control spirit is a form of witchcraft, regardless of who does it.

[The following excerpts are adapted from *Overcoming Evil in the Last Days.*]

# Wisdom Over Witchcraft Reflections

**B**ECAUSE witchcraft is counterfeit spiritual authority, we will only be completely free from the power of witchcraft when we are completely submitted to the authority of God. If the spiritual void that is in us is not filled with the real power and authority of God, we will become subject to witchcraft in some form as we draw closer to the end of the age.

The Battle of Armageddon is fought in the *"valley of decision"* ( Joel 3:14); everyone on earth will be brought to the place of making a decision. It is a powerful confrontation, and the choice will be made concerning issues of power and authority. We will choose either the power and authority of God or the power and authority of the evil one—but we will all choose.

Those who are the target of any form of witchcraft will usually feel the sequence of stings [confusion; depression; loss of vision; disorientation; withdrawal; despair; defeat]. If we react to the attack properly, we will not only be free of its influence ourselves, but we can also help to free those who have used witchcraft. Spirits gain entrance through fear. Those who are fearful and insecure are so obsessed with controlling others that they use evil influence, and it will take a demonstration of *"perfect love"* (1 John 4:18) to cast out these fears. Jesus commanded us to *"bless those who curse you"* (Matt. 5:44 NKJV). Paul said that we are not to return evil for evil; we are to overcome evil with good (see Rom. 12:19-21).

Witchcraft is a serious offense that God will not continue to tolerate in the Church. His intent is to bring down every form and manifestation of witchcraft that ensnares His people. After we have been freed from this terrible evil, we will also be free to walk in the unprecedented power He will entrust to those who walk in true spiritual authority.

The only yoke that we must take is the Lord's yoke. His yoke is easy and His burden is light (see Matt. 11:28-30).

# *Points to Ponder*

Using manipulation or a control spirit is a form of witchcraft, regardless of who does it.

Because witchcraft is counterfeit spiritual authority, you will only be completely free from the power of witchcraft when you are completely submitted to the authority of God.

If the spiritual void that is in you is not filled with the real power and authority of God, you will become subject to witchcraft in some form as you draw closer to the end of the age.

A demonstration of "perfect love" will cast out fears.

After you have been freed from this terrible evil, you will also be free to walk in the unprecedented power He will entrust to those who walk in true spiritual authority.

# *Words of Wisdom*

God is using every circumstance of life to conform you to His image. It is the enemy who comes to kill, steal, and destroy, but God uses what is intended for evil and turns it for your good. If you have been murmuring and complaining about your emotional hurts, stop right now and ask God to forgive you.

—Morris Cerullo, *You Can Have a New Beginning*[1]

*There shall not be found among you anyone who makes his son or his daughter pass through the fire, one who uses divination, one who practices witchcraft, or one who interprets omens, or a sorcerer* (Deuteronomy 18:10).

To deny the possibility, nay, the actual existence of witchcraft and sorcery, is at once flatly to contradict the revealed word of God in various passages both of the Old and New Testament, and the thing itself is a Truth to which every nation in the world hath, in its turn, borne testimony, by either example seemingly well attested or by prohibitory laws, which at least suppose the possibility of a commerce with evil spirits.

—Sir William Blackstone[2]

Like millions of others, I got pulled into the wonders of Hogwarts School of Witchcraft and Wizardry and the drama of Harry discovering his powers and unexpected destiny.

—Kurt Bruner, *The Twilight Phenomenon*[3]

# My Wisdom Keys

_____

_____

_____

_____

_____

_____

_____

_____

_____

_____

_____

_____

_____

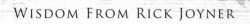

# 22

# *Wisdom Over a Religious Spirit*

A religious spirit is a demon that seeks to substitute religious activity for the power of the Holy Spirit in our lives. Its primary objective is to have the Church *"holding to a form of godliness, although they have denied its power"* (2 Tim. 3:5). The apostle Paul completed his exhortation with *"avoid such men as these."* This religious spirit is the *"leaven of the Pharisees and Sadducees"* (Matt. 16:6) of which the Lord warned His disciples to beware.

[The following excerpts are adapted from *Overcoming Evil in the Last Days.*]

# Wisdom Over a Religious Spirit Reflections

HE Lord often used metaphors to illustrate the lessons He taught. The religious spirit operates like the leaven in bread, which does not add substance or nutritional value to the bread—it only inflates it. Such is the byproduct of the religious spirit. It does not add to the life or power of the Church; it merely feeds the very pride of man that caused the first fall and almost every fall since.

Satan seems to understand even better than the Church that *"God resists the proud, but gives grace to the humble"* (James 4:6 NKJV). He knows very well that God will not inhabit any work that is inflated with pride and that God Himself will even resist such a work. Satan's strategy is to make us proud—even proud of good things, such as how much we read our Bibles, witness, or feed the poor. He knows that, if we do the will of God in pride, our work will be counterproductive and could even ultimately work toward our fall.

Satan also knows that, once leaven gets into the bread, it is extremely difficult to remove. Pride, by its very nature, is the most difficult stronghold to remove or correct. A religious spirit keeps us from hearing the voice of God by encouraging us to assume that we already know God's opinion, what He is saying, and what pleases Him. This delusion is the result of believing that God is just like us. A religious spirit encourages the rationalization of Scripture, having us believe that rebukes, exhortations, and words of correction are for other people but not for us.

We will never have the authority to deliver others from darkness until we are free from it ourselves. To begin taking ground from this vast enemy, we must ask the Lord to shine His light on us, showing how this applies to us personally. As illustrated by the Lord's continual confrontations with the Pharisees, the Church's most desperate fight from the very beginning has been with this spirit. Just as the primary characteristic of the Pharisees was focusing on what was wrong with others while being blind to their own faults, the religious spirit tries to make us do the same.

# Points to Ponder

A religious spirit is a demon that seeks to substitute religious activity for the power of the Holy Spirit in your life.

Satan knows very well that God will not inhabit any work that is inflated with pride and that God Himself will even resist such a work.

Satan's strategy is to make you proud—even proud of good things, such as how much you read your Bible, witness, or feed the poor.

Satan knows that, if you do the will of God in pride, your work will be counterproductive and could even ultimately work toward your fall.

To begin taking ground from this vast enemy, you must ask the Lord to shine His light on you, showing how this applies to you personally.

# *Words of Wisdom*

A dark heart is a heart that is unable to perceive spiritual reality. It is unmoved by the desires and affections of the Lord, and therefore cannot respond to His invitation to relationship, which is the source of life. As Paul explains in Romans chapter 1, a dark heart perverts our desires and leads us into all kinds of sin that degrades our identity and relationships.

—Bill Johnson, *Strengthen Yourself in the Lord*[1]

*Pride goes before destruction, and a haughty spirit before stumbling* (Proverbs 16:18).

My wife and I have taken this principle [service to others] to heart and have ministered to tens of thousands of at-risk children since 1981. Then when the time came to lead the fight against same-sex marriage in our city, we had already earned a place of respect because of the service we had freely given to our community.

—Joseph Mattera, *Kingdom Revolution*[2]

God despises pride. Pride usually leads into a terrible fall. Only Satan can convince us that we, by our own strength, have accomplished anything good spiritually.

—Curtis C. Thomas, *Practical Wisdom for Pastors*[3]

# MY WISDOM KEYS

_____

_____

_____

_____

_____

_____

_____

_____

_____

_____

_____

_____

_____

_____

# 23

# *Wisdom's Ultimate Battle*

Basic to understanding the biblical prophecies of our times is the Lord's statement in Matthew 13:39: *"The harvest is the end of the age."* As He makes clear in His other parables and statements about the end of the age, this harvest is the reaping of everything that has been sown in man, both the good and the evil. Both are coming to full maturity. The righteous will become more righteous, and the wicked more wicked. Therefore, at the end of the age we will have the ultimate battle between good and evil.

[The following excerpts are adapted from *Delivered From Evil*.]

# Wisdom's Ultimate Battle Reflections

IT is for this reason that we must put on the full armor that has been given to us by God and learn how to use our divinely powerful weapons effectively. Two of the most powerful weapons that we have been given are love and truth. Therefore, a most basic goal of our life should be to walk in love and truth in all that we do. As we are told in Romans 12:21: *"Do not be overcome by evil, but overcome evil with good."*

Basically, we overcome every evil released on the earth by growing in God's counterpower to it. We overcome the fear being released on the earth by walking in faith. We overcome hatred and wrath by growing in love. We overcome rebellion and lawlessness by growing in obedience and devotion to the Lordship of Jesus. In this way we discern the evil that is growing in the world and overcome it by ourselves growing in God's grace that counters it.

The Lord does not want us to go out of the world, or He would have already taken us out of it. There are relationships that we need and should have with unbelievers in order to be a witness to them. However, we do need to refrain from covenant relationship with unbelievers. That is what it means to be "bound together." Those who are bound together with unbelievers are going to be increasingly torn between one camp or the other, and at some point, trying to live in both worlds will no longer be possible.

166

We must also be aware of the fact that unifying, for either good or evil, does increase power. As in the parable of the wheat and tares, the evil is gathered into bundles first, and as stated, evil has in fact been unifying more and faster than the Church until now. This is why evil has seemed more powerful and has been advancing far more than the Kingdom in many places. Even so, we are now coming to the time when the wheat will start gathering together, coming into unity, and therefore growing in power. The tide of evil will then be turned, which is already happening in many places.

# *Points to Ponder*

At the end of the age there will be an ultimate battle between good and evil.

Two of the most powerful weapons that you have been given are love and truth.

A most basic goal of your life should be to walk in love and truth in all that you do.

The Lord does not want you to go out of the world or He would have already taken you out of it.

There are relationships that you need and should have with unbelievers in order to be a witness to them, but refrain from covenant relationships with unbelievers.

# *Words of Wisdom*

*Out of the ground the Lord God caused to grow every
tree that is pleasing to the sight and good for food; the tree
of life also in the midst of the garden, and the tree of the
knowledge of good and evil* (Genesis 2:9).

Someone once said, "The problem with life is that it is so
*daily.*" I agree! Many of us have great ideas about life, about
what it should be like and how we can become successful at
it. But for most of us, the struggle lies in daily walking out our
convictions—especially when it comes to thinking in such a
way that our *minds* don't violate our *hearts*.

—Kris Vallotton, *Sexual Revolution*[1]

*Do not be overcome by evil, but overcome evil with good*
(Romans 12:21).

The modern environmentalist usually considers what is natural
as good. In contrast, the Christian should determine his or her
ethics based on what Jesus Christ says is right and what He
says is wrong, because on judgment day only His ethics will be
relevant.

—Harold R. Eberle, *Christianity Unshackled*[2]

# MY WISDOM KEYS

# 24

## *Wisdom, Redemption, and Restoration*

The most basic purpose of God on the earth is redemption and restoration. If you take the first three chapters of the Bible, and the last three, you have a complete story. Everything between those six chapters deals with one basic subject: the redemption and restoration of man, and the domain that had been given to man, from the Fall.

[The following excerpts are adapted from *Delivered From Evil*.]

# Wisdom, Redemption, and Restoration Reflections

I N the apostle Peter's second sermon, he made a very important statement about the Lord's return, saying, *"Whom heaven must receive until the period of restoration of all things about which God spoke by the mouth of His holy prophets from ancient time"* (Acts 3:21). The "all things" that will be restored is, of course, all that was lost after the Fall. There will be a complete restoration of humans and all that was under Adam's domain that has likewise been subject to the consequences of the Fall. This period of restoration that Peter is talking about here is the reign of Christ on the earth, which we are coming to.

Of course, the Church is called to reign with Him during this period. After the Lord's death and resurrection, the Church became the ultimate vehicle for this ultimate purpose on the earth. This whole age has actually been "training for reigning" for those who are called to be members of His household. The purpose of this reign is restoration. Restoration is, therefore, one of the most important things that we learn.

The first and most important thing that was lost by the Fall was the intimate fellowship that man had with God. The main purpose of redemption and restoration is to restore that relationship. If there is any way that we can determine the degree to which redemption and restoration has truly worked in our life, it would be by how close to God we have become.

The second most basic thing that was lost by the Fall was the depth and quality of the fellowship that man was to have with his fellow man. Remember, the very first thing that God said that was not good was for man to be alone, or loneliness. This was said when man had God, so we can conclude that man was created to need more than just his fellowship with God—he also needed fellowship with other people. He created us to be social beings.

When the Church really becomes what it is called to be, the whole world will yearn to be part of such a fellowship.

# *Points to Ponder*

The most basic purpose of God on the earth is
redemption and restoration.

After the Lord's death and resurrection, the Church became
the ultimate vehicle for this ultimate purpose on the earth.

If there is any way that you can determine the degree to
which redemption and restoration has truly worked in your
life, it would be by how close to God you have become.

Humankind was created to need more than just your
fellowship with God—you also need fellowship
with other people.

# *Words of Wisdom*

One woman was healed from colon cancer while dancing before the Lord. Another woman had endured several surgeries on her shoulder trying to resolve the constant pain issues. As she worshiped the Lord, the Holy Spirit touched her shoulder, and she immediately removed the sling she had been wearing for five months because she was healed!

—Sid Roth, *The Incomplete Church*[1]

*In Him we have redemption through His blood, the forgiveness of our trespasses, according to the riches of His grace which He lavished on us* (Ephesians 1:7-8).

In Amos 9:11, the Lord promises in the last days to restore David's fallen tent and to repair its broken places and restore its ruins and build it as it used to be!

—Charles P. Schmitt,
*End-Time Truths for End-Time People*[2]

# MY WISDOM KEYS

# 25

# *Wisdom Overcomes Rebellion*

The most basic evil is rebellion against God. That is what released all of the death into the world in the first place, and it is basically what will cause all of the death and destruction in our times. The ultimate lesson that all of creation will learn from what comes upon the world at the end is the consequence of thinking that we can do anything without God. Man was created to need God, and we do need Him. We will make a terrible mess out of anything that we do without Him.

[The following excerpts are adapted from *Delivered From Evil.*]

# Wisdom Overcomes Rebellion Reflections

THE death and destruction that comes upon the world at the end is not so much the result of God hurling His judgments at the world, as it is the consequences of man's own behavior. A basic spiritual principle is stated in Galatians 6:7: *"Do not be deceived, God is not mocked; for whatever a man sows, this he will also reap."* Everyone will reap what he or she sows. Much of the destruction that comes at the end is simply the consequences of man's own rebellion and determination to live without God.

The ultimate state of rebellion is known as "lawlessness." That basically means to be without principles or moral code. That is precisely the state that the wicked are coming to. In contrast to this, the righteous will get more righteous. Their integrity, their moral code, will get stronger and stronger—so will their obedience to the Lord.

Satan's ultimate purpose is to declare to the entire creation of God that man, the crown jewel of God's creation, loves satan and his ways more than God and His ways. Presently, satan can point to the Church and boast that even Christians love sin more than they love righteousness. However, when a person is obedient to God and resists the overwhelming temptations and pressures of this world to do evil, and instead remains faithful to God and obedient to Him, that person becomes a witness to even principalities and powers in the heavenly realm.

Therefore, the ultimate test will be to live in obedience and faithfulness to God or fall into the ranks of lawlessness. Because love is the greatest force behind good, only those who truly love God will remain faithful. This is why the Lord stated in Matthew 24:12-13: *"Because lawlessness is increased, most people's love will grow cold. But the one who endures to the end, he will be saved."*

One of the things that we can be sure of at the end is that "most" Christians' love will grow cold, and it will be eroded because of lawlessness. Therefore, lawlessness is one of the ultimate tests that we can expect to try our hearts at the end.

We must, therefore, be vigilant to watch over our hearts. Begin to ask now what is happening to our love. If it is not getting stronger, it is getting weaker. Is our love for God being eroded by the lawlessness that is increasing? Read Romans 6:19-23 for the answer.

# *Points to Ponder*

The most basic evil is rebellion against God.

The death and destruction that comes upon the world at the end is not so much the result of God hurling His judgments at the world, as it is the consequences of your own behavior.

Do you love satan and his ways more than God and His ways?

When you are obedient to God and resist the overwhelming temptations and pressures of this world to do evil, and instead remain faithful to God and obedient to Him, you become a witness to even principalities and powers in the heavenly realm.

# *Words of Wisdom*

The beginning of men's rebellion against God was, and is, the lack of a thankful heart.

—Francis Schaeffer

*But that prophet or that dreamer of dreams shall be put to death, because he has counseled rebellion against the Lord your God who brought you from the land of Egypt and redeemed you from the house of slavery, to seduce you from the way in which the Lord your God commanded you to walk. So you shall purge the evil from among you* (Deuteronomy 13:5).

Much sickness—physical, mental, and emotional—surely must come from disobedience. When the soul is confronted with an alternative of right or wrong and chooses to blur the distinction, making excuses for its bewilderment and frustration, it is exposed to infection. Evil is given the opportunity to invade the mind, the spirit, and the body and the sick person goes off to an expert who will diagnose his trouble. Sometimes the patient knows well what his trouble is and for this very reason has not consulted the Lord, fearing what He will say: confess. Turn around. Quit that indulgence. Do not pity yourself. Forgive that person. Pay back what you owe. Apologize. Tell the truth. Deny yourself. Consider the other's well-being. Lay down your life.

—Elisabeth Elliot, *Discipline: The Glad Surrender*[1]

# MY WISDOM KEYS

_____

_____

_____

_____

_____

_____

_____

_____

_____

_____

_____

_____

_____

# 26

# *Wisdom, Not Confusion*

Confusion is one of the most devastating enemies of truth and human achievement. Confusion can cripple the most brilliant, or the most diligent. For this reason, getting free from confusion can make one of the most radical changes in a person's life, turning it from one of defeat and depression into a life of joy, peace, and fruitfulness. Therefore, recognizing and overcoming the spirit of confusion is essential for all who desire to walk in their destiny and accomplish their purpose.

[The following excerpts are adapted from *Delivered From Evil.*]

# Wisdom, Not Confusion
## Reflections

LIVING with confusion is like being in a thick fog every day. Many become so accustomed to this that they do not even know that they are living in a state of confusion. Like children with poor eyesight who put on glasses for the first time, they are astonished at the world around them when they break out from under this terrible oppression. As Proverbs 4:18 states, *"But the path of the righteous is like the light of dawn, that shines brighter and brighter until the full day."* Every Christian should live by a light in their life that gets brighter every day. If this is not the case for you, then there is a good possibility that in some way you have departed from the path that you were called to walk, and by this opened the door to confusion.

However, be encouraged because this can be corrected almost as quickly as the child with poor eyesight who puts on a pair of prescription glasses. Just as this child will immediately see the world differently, when you break the power of confusion off your life, you too will start to see the world clearly. You will immediately begin to live with a new decisiveness, a confidence, and a peace that others will probably see as miraculous. As a Christian you are not called to live in confusion, but to walk in a light that not only makes your own path clear, but also reveals the path of light to others who are walking in darkness. You must not settle for anything less.

Obviously, confusion can range in power and degree. It can work to keep us from understanding a single matter clearly, but it can also be so pervasive that it keeps us from understanding almost anything clearly. Even if our state of confusion seems relatively mild, we must resolve not to allow any of it in our life. Once confusion gets a foothold into just one part of our life, it will begin to undermine our faith and our confidence, and eventually it will spill over into other areas of our life. Its goal is the complete disruption of our life. Confusion wants to hinder our progress in everything. If it is not cut off at its root, like a weed it will come back and multiply. This is why our goal must be to understand the roots of confusion and learn to pull it out by its roots so that it cannot come back or spread.

# *Points to Ponder*

Recognizing and overcoming the spirit of confusion is essential if you desire to walk in your destiny and accomplish your purpose.

Do you live by a light in your life that gets brighter every day?

If this is not the case for you, then there is a good possibility that in some way you have departed from the path that you were called to walk, and by this opened the door to confusion.

Once confusion gets a foothold into just one part of your life, it will undermine your faith and your confidence, and eventually it will spill over into other areas of your life.

Determine to understand the roots of confusion and pull it out by its roots.

# Words of Wisdom

*For God is not a God of confusion but of peace*
(1 Corinthians 14:33).

Just when we think we know everything, God comes along and uses that which we think is not useful. It is amazing how the one we judge or give up on is the very same person God will reach out to. I was one of those people. I was a Muslim....

—Faisal Malick, *The Destiny of Islam in the Endtimes*[1]

Four things to learn in life: To think clearly without hurry or confusion. To love everybody sincerely. To act in everything with the highest motives. To trust God unhesitatingly.

—Helen Keller

Then in 1974 God revealed to me the main reason why I couldn't understand the Bible. He showed me that I had an idol in my life. That idol was my career. It was more important to me than God.

—Richard Booker, *The Miracle of the Scarlet Thread*[2]

# MY WISDOM KEYS

---
---
---
---
---
---
---
---
---
---
---
---
---
---

# 27

# *Wisdom and Trust*

It is tragic the way that skepticism is now viewed as a foundation for wisdom and necessary for the pursuit of truth. Skepticism is the foundation of a darkened soul, an open door to the devil's heart, and is contrary to faith that is the foundation of a genuine pursuit of truth. In First Corinthians 13:7 we are told that love *"believes all things, hopes all things...."* This does not mean that love is naïve, or that it does not see flaws and mistakes. What it does mean is that love looks for the best in others, and hopes for the best, not the worst. If you are examining another, looking for the worst in them, you can be sure that the devil will show it to you, and bend it considerably as he does.

[The following excerpts are adapted from *Delivered From Evil*.]

# Wisdom and Trust Reflections

**Y**OU may think that anyone who lives by the mandate of love in First Corinthians 13 will suffer perpetual disappointment and perpetual hurt. That is very possible. One thing that few realize, and that every Christian needs to settle in their heart and mind, is that being hurt by others is basic to the call of being a Christian. To live in a way that tries to avoid being hurt will divert us from our basic calling and the path of righteousness.

One of the greatest demonstrations of true love is to keep believing in someone after they have disappointed you or hurt you. We are called to take up our cross daily. The cross is the symbol of the greatest injustice that the world has ever witnessed. No one ever deserved the persecution and death that He suffered less than Jesus did. Yet, He came into this world knowing that this was going to happen, and willingly went to the cross for our salvation. He said in John 17:18, concerning those whom He had called, *"As You sent Me into the world, I also have sent them into the world."* We have actually been sent into the world to experience injustice and yet, like our Savior, to keep on loving and believing in people.

How many of us would earnestly desire to have one more meal with our closest friends if we knew that within hours these people whom we have invested so much in would deny that they even knew us? It is the basic nature of love to love regardless of how those we love return it. This is the way that we are also called to walk.

Possibly the greatest simplifying factor in our lives would be to let love be our motive in all things in place of the self-interests that usually motivate us. This would so simplify our lives because the Lord promises that if we will seek His interests first, which is His Kingdom, He will take care of everything that concerns us (see Matt. 6:31-34).

There is no greater freedom that we can ever know than to be dead to this world. What can you do to a dead man? It is impossible for a dead man to be offended, feel rejected or sorry for himself, or even get angry. It is impossible for a dead man to be confused. If these things are still happening to us, it is only evidence to the degree that we have refused to walk in our most basic calling as Christians—to take up our crosses (die to ourselves) and follow Him.

# *Points to Ponder*

Trusting in love finds the best in others and hopes for the best, not the worst.

To live in a way that avoids being hurt diverts you from your basic calling and the path of righteousness.

Would you honestly want to have a last meal with your closest friends if you knew that within hours they would deny that they even knew you?

Possibly the greatest simplifying factor in your life is to trust in love and allow love to be your motive.

There is no greater freedom than being dead to this world.

# *Words of Wisdom*

*Trust in the Lord with all your heart and do not lean on your own understanding. In all your ways acknowledge Him, and He will make your paths straight* (Proverbs 3:5-6).

There is no secret formula to build trust, and there's no magical principle to learn to trust God. Trust is built on relationship. God wants a healthy relationship with you; He wants you to trust Him. The answer lies with you.

—Elmer L. Towns, *How God Answers Prayer*[1]

Trusting God with your successes isn't really a challenge. The real test of trust is to be able to share your secrets, your inner failures, and your fears.

—T.D. Jakes, *40 Days of Power*[2]

The Lord watched me and waited for me to recover from that most wonderful revelation. "Religion is satisfied for you to look like Me and act like Me. The outer appearance is everything to that system. But from the beginning, it was not to be this way. From the beginning, there would be a people who would yield to Me, trust Me, love Me.

—Don Nori, *The Love Shack*[3]

# MY WISDOM KEYS

_____

_____

_____

_____

_____

_____

_____

_____

_____

_____

_____

_____

_____

_____

# 28

## *Wisdom to Meet Needs*

When Jesus told His disciples who were looking at 5,000 hungry people, "You give them something to eat," He empowered them to do it, multiplying their resources. When He directs us to meet anyone's needs, He will empower us to do it, and when He does this we can count on our resources going a lot further than if we try to do it on our own.

Of course, many are asking how do we know the ones that the Lord is leading us to help. Simple—we have to know His voice. Remember, His sheep follow Him because they know His voice (see John 10:4). Getting to know His voice is not complicated. It is based on simply spending time with Him.

[The following excerpts are adapted from *Delivered From Evil*.]

# Wisdom to Meet Needs Reflections

LET us also understand that when we determine not to be controlled by other people's expectations, but rather by the love of Christ, this does not mean that we rebel against our boss because we are not going to let his expectations control us. We must endeavor to live by Colossians 3:23-24:

> *Whatever you do, do your work heartily, as for the Lord rather than for men, knowing that from the Lord you will receive the reward of the inheritance. It is the Lord Christ whom you serve.*

If we have made the commitment to take a job, we will therefore seek in every way to do the best possible job because of our love for the Lord—whom we are ultimately working for—and because of the love that He has given to us for the people we work for and with.

If we love others, we will also be understanding of why they may not react to us with consistency. We will have an understanding of the confusion in this world that they are having to constantly battle. We will therefore endeavor to be consistent in our relationship to them whether they are or not. This we do because of our love for them, and love *loves* whether it is rewarded or not. Therefore our goal in all of our relationships should be the simplicity of love that does not waver, even when it is at times rejected or hurt.

As we begin to walk in the consistency that comes from following the One in whom there is no inconsistency or shadow of turning, we will become a rock of refuge in the midst of the storms of confusion in this world. Others will trust us more and more, and this trust can become a bridge by which we can help them to find deliverance through Christ. We must also consider that the more confusion and inconsistency that we are faced with in a relationship, the greater the opportunity that we have to demonstrate the love of God that does not waver.

# *Points to Ponder*

When God directs you to meet anyone's needs, He will empower you to do it. When He does, you can count on your resources going a lot further than if you try to do it on your own.

If you have made the commitment to take a job, you should do the best possible job because of your love for the Lord.

Your goal in all of your relationships should be the simplicity of love that does not waver, even when it is at times rejected or hurt.

As you walk in the consistency that comes from following the One in whom there is no inconsistency, you will become a rock of refuge in the midst of the storms of confusion in this world.

# *Words of Wisdom*

*"For I was hungry, and you gave Me something to eat; I was thirsty, and you gave Me something to drink; I was a stranger, and you invited Me in; naked, and you clothed Me; I was sick, and you visited Me; I was in prison, and you came to Me." Then the righteous will answer Him, "Lord, when did we see You hungry, and feed You, or thirsty, and give You something to drink? And when did we see You a stranger, and invite You in, or naked, and clothe You? When did we see You sick, or in prison, and come to You?" The King will answer and say to them, "Truly I say to you, to the extent that you did it to one of these brothers of Mine, even the least of them, you did it to Me"* (Matthew 25:35-40).

In this life we cannot do great things. We can only do small things with great love.

—Mother Teresa

He is the kind of person who loves people enough to accept them as they are, yet is willing to risk the pushback that comes when the truth is spoken in love.

—Donna Scuderi, *Reflections on 90 Minutes in Heaven*[1]

## MY WISDOM KEYS

# 29

# *Wisdom Over Pride*

Pride is one of the biggest open doors to confusion. As we are told in Proverbs 11:2, *"When pride comes, then comes dishonor, but with the humble is wisdom."* If we are to walk in the honor and dignity of our calling, we must begin with having the humility to know how desperately we are dependent on the grace and redemption of God that is available to us at the cross. To walk in the light and to be able to see where we are going will require humility. We must start to recognize this deadly enemy—pride—and repent of it.

[The following excerpts are adapted from *Delivered From Evil.*]

# Wisdom Over Pride Reflections

THE main reason that we usually refuse to acknowledge a problem is pride, and this is the pride that will even cause God to resist us. As Peter Lord likes to say, "The main thing is to keep the main thing the main thing," and the main thing we need in our life is God's grace. Since He gives grace to the humble, pursuing humility is one of the most worthwhile devotions we can have.

Many of the complications in most people's lives are the direct result of pride. For this reason, in many cases confusion will start to be dispelled the moment we determine to humble ourselves in a matter. When we catch this truth, as well as the even more important one that God gives His grace to the humble, we will begin to spend much more time seeking to humble ourselves than we do trying to exalt ourselves like we usually do. This alone can send great clouds of darkness fleeing. Those who start to know the true value of the grace and favor of God will not care at all what they look like before people—their pursuit will be the grace of God that comes with humility. In fact, as this truth becomes a reality to us, we will start devoting much more time to looking smaller, trying to humble ourselves every opportunity that we get.

Just being a Christian in this world requires a certain amount of humility. The pride that most of the people of this world live by compels them to think that belief in God is a crutch. I fully agree that it is because I know that I need a crutch. In fact, at the end of this age things will be in such a mess that all of humanity, and the rest of creation, will know for sure that we cannot run things without God—we need Him! I thank Him daily that He is willing to be our crutch!

The pride of man in such forms as humanism is the source of some of the darkest forms of confusion on the earth. It was a nationalistic pride that led some of the world's most noble and brilliant people, the Germans, to fall to the tragic delusions of the Nazis. Such pride will open the door to delusions in our churches, our companies, and even our families. Any good that we are or have that does not acknowledge it as being the grace of God will be a wide open door for delusion and deception.

# *Points to Ponder*

To walk in the light and to be able to see where you are going requires humility.

Do you recognize the deadly enemy—pride— and repent of it?

Pursuing humility is one of the most worthwhile devotions you can have.

Pride in such forms as humanism is the source of some of the darkest forms of confusion on the earth.

Is God your crutch?

# *Words of Wisdom*

*When pride comes, then comes dishonor, but with the humble is wisdom* (Proverbs 11:2).

Step 1. Free yourself from pride. Evidences of pride include: failure to admit mistakes, lack of a teachable spirit, self-centered conversation, a bossy attitude.

—Terry Nance, *God's Armorbearer*[1]

Pride is the worst viper in the human heart! Pride is the greatest disturber of the soul's peace, and of sweet communion with Christ. Pride is with the greatest difficulty rooted out. Pride is the most hidden, secret, and deceitful of all lusts! Pride often creeps insensibly into the midst of religion, even, sometimes, under the disguise of humility itself!

—Jonathan Edwards

There are two words that don't go together: pride and Christian. How can you be a proud Christian? That's an oxymoron. The opposite is true. Becoming a Christian requires humility; humility to say, "God, I'm a sinner. I don't deserve Heaven.... You, in Your rich mercy, have forgiven me, a wretched sinner. God, thank You."

—Bob Lenz, *Grace*[2]

# MY WISDOM KEYS

# 30

## *Wisdom's Light*

Without light, we could not see. Light makes all things manifest. After the Spirit moved, His first great task was to bring forth light. Light represents truth, and as soon as the Lord begins to move in our lives, His first task will be to shine the light of His truth into our lives.

It is interesting to note that light was created before the sun, moon, and the stars—which were not created until the fourth day of creation—before the vessels that were to manifest it. Jesus is the Light of the world, and He existed as One with God before the world. We see this in John's great explanation of Jesus at the beginning of his Gospel (see John 1:1-4;9-12).

[The following excerpts are adapted from *Unshakable Faith*.]

# Wisdom's Light Reflections

"IN Him all things hold together" (Col. 1:17) reveals that Jesus is the binding force in all of creation. The light was created before the sun, moon, and stars as an eternal testimony that He must be given first place in everything. Every new believer needs to be saturated with the revelation of who Jesus is before their attention is turned to all of the other doctrines of the faith, or an understanding of their place in the Church. The Light, Jesus, must have preeminence in all things. He is the first, and He is the last. Jesus is the Light of God, and all things will be summed up in Him. We must know Him first.

First John 1:7 makes clear that if we depart from fellowship, we also depart from His light. If we break fellowship with His people, we will also be breaking fellowship with Him. Christianity without fellowship is not true Christianity. The Lord created His Church so we would all need one another. No one will get to their destination in Christ alone.

Church life can be one of the most glorious—and most difficult—experiences we can have. Amos 3:3 states, *"Can two walk together, except they be agreed?"* (KJV). This does not imply that we must agree on everything to walk together, but we walk together in the things upon which we do agree. Every Christian agrees that Jesus Christ is Lord, so every Christian can walk together to some degree. There should be at least some level of fellowship between all who hold to the basic truths of the faith.

As we walk together, understanding and agreement will grow. To have fellowship, we must start by looking for things upon which we agree, rather than those upon which we disagree. This will enable us to stay in the light, which requires that we *"have fellowship with one another"* (1 John 1:7). Likewise, when we start breaking off fellowship with God's people, we will start walking in darkness. We cannot be joined to Jesus Christ without also being joined to His Body, the Church.

# *Points to Ponder*

Light represents truth, and when the Lord moves in your life, He shines the light of His truth into your life.

Jesus is the Light of God, and all things are summed up in Him. You must know Him first.

Every Christian agrees that Jesus Christ is Lord, so every Christian can walk together to some degree.

To have fellowship, you must start by looking for things upon which you agree, rather than those upon which you disagree.

As you walk together with others, understanding and agreement grows.

# *Words of Wisdom*

A wandering star has no fixed relationship. People who are like wandering stars have no fixed relationships with other Christians. Nobody is guiding them. Even if they start out as truly anointed, they get off track when they stop being accountable to peers who can speak into their lives.

—Mickey Robinson, *The Prophetic Made Personal*[1]

We are called to walk in victory in the name of Jesus. This is not an impossible dream! It is a reality, but only if we put God first.

—Sharon L. Grant, *Giving Up Is Not an Option*[2]

People travel to wonder at the height of the mountains, at the huge waves of the seas, at the long course of the rivers, at the vast compass of the ocean, at the circular motion of the stars, and yet they pass by themselves without wondering.

—Augustine

People are like stained-glass windows. They sparkle and shine when the sun is out, but when the darkness sets in their true beauty is revealed only if there is light from within.

—Elisabeth Kübler-Ross

# MY WISDOM KEYS

_____

_____

_____

_____

_____

_____

_____

_____

_____

_____

_____

_____

_____

# 31

## *Wisdom of Life*

The Lord said that His people were worth *"more than many sparrows"* (Matt. 10:31 NIV), so sparrows are obviously worth something to Him. When He created the beasts, He *"saw that it was good"* (Gen. 1:25). The creation is precious to the Lord, which is why we see in Revelation 11:18 that when the Lord's great wrath comes at the end, one reason is *"to destroy those who destroy the earth."*

Christians should be the most devoted conservationists of all, counting precious what our wonderful Creator has given us to enjoy on the earth. Life, in all its forms, must be esteemed and protected. However, this must not be confused with the idolatrous worship of the creation in place of the Creator.

[The following excerpts are adapted from *Unshakable Faith*.]

# Wisdom of Life Reflections

JESUS came to lead us in the path of life. In Him is life, and He is the One with the words of life. If we are abiding in Him, life should likewise be flowing from us. We have been given a well of living water that will never run dry. In all that we do, we should love, seek, preserve, and spread life.

One of the most ancient philosophical questions is: What is life? In simplified terms, life is communication. We have life for as long as we can communicate, or interrelate, with our environment. Man is called a "higher form of life" because we communicate on a higher level. We are likewise alive spiritually only if we communicate spiritually. As the Lord said in John 6:63, *"The words that I have spoken to you are spirit and are life."* We only have spiritual life if we hear His words, or communicate on a spiritual level. If we are alive in the Spirit, then they can kill our bodies but they cannot take our lives. As He said in John 11:25-26, *"I am the resurrection and the life; he who believes in Me will live even if he dies, and everyone who lives and believes in Me will never die."*

In Scripture, our spirits are sometimes referred to as our heart. That is why we read in Proverbs 4:23, *"Watch over your heart with all diligence, for from it flow the springs of life."* The Lord explained in Luke 6:45 that *"the good man out of the good treasure of his heart brings forth what is good; and the evil man out of the evil treasure brings forth what is evil; for his mouth*

214

*speaks from that which fills his heart."* We quoted before from Proverbs 18:21, *"Death and life are in the power of the tongue, and those who love it will eat its fruit."* As a famous statesman once said, "Let your words be sweet because you never know when you may have to eat them!"

Our words are an indication of what is in our hearts. Proverbs 10:11 states, *"The mouth of the righteous is a fountain of life."* As James wrote, *"Does a fountain send out from the same opening both fresh and bitter water?"* (James 3:11). Amazing, but true, our words can actually have the power of life or death in them. The words of the Gospel preached can actually have the seed of eternal life in them. Let us always guard our words so that they impart life.

# Points to Ponder

Christians should be the most devoted conservationists of all, counting precious what your wonderful Creator has given you to enjoy on the earth.

Life, in all of its forms, must be esteemed and protected.

If you are abiding in Him, life should likewise be flowing from you.

You have been given a well of living water that will never run dry.

Guard your words so they impart life to others.

# Words of Wisdom

Certainly every Christian ought to be praying and working to nullify the abominable abortion law. But as we work and pray, we should have in mind not only this important issue as though it stood alone. Rather, we should be struggling and praying that this whole other total entity *"(this godless) worldview"* can be rolled back with all its results across all of life.

—Francis Schaeffer, *A Christian Manifesto*[1]

Ethics, too, are nothing but reverence for life. This is what gives me the fundamental principle of morality, namely, that good consists in maintaining, promoting, and enhancing life, and that destroying, injuring, and limiting life are evil.

—Albert Schweitzer

The relationship of eternal life with God is built on trust in the One who offers it freely. Life in the Kingdom flows forth from the King. His life is resurrection life that knows no limits.

—Mark Van Deman, *A Traveler's Guide to the Spirit Realm*[2]

And in the end, it's not the years in your life that count. It's the life in your years.

—Abraham Lincoln

# My Wisdom Keys

_____

_____

_____

_____

_____

_____

_____

_____

_____

_____

_____

_____

_____

# 32

## *Wisdom of Diversity*

The Lord so loves diversity that He made every snowflake different. He made every tree and person different. His creativity continues to expand with every new plant or creature that is brought forth. Even when Jesus walked the earth, He never healed people the same way twice. In every new setting He had a different message. There is a newness and freshness to God every day. Walking with Him is to be in a continual state of awe and marvel. Yet, the foundation of this exploding creativity is set within boundaries that allow it to flow in a beautiful and orderly symmetry, not chaos.

[The following excerpts are adapted from *Unshakable Faith*.]

# Wisdom of Diversity Reflections

**T**HOSE who are becoming like the Lord will obviously love creativity. Those who know the blessed Creator, and are becoming like Him, should be creative. We should love diversity, and yet respect order and purpose. When properly combined, we will be much closer to becoming like Him.

If we have His heart for diversity and creativity, whenever we meet someone who is different from us, we will be open and expectant of learning something, not closed and fearful. One of the distinguishing characteristics between the "sheep and goats" is when the Lord came to them as a stranger, and the sheep took Him in (see Matt. 25:32-36). The Greek word translated "stranger" is *xenos* (xen'-os), which is literally a "foreigner or alien." The Lord often comes to us through those who are different from us. If we are not open to them, we will not be open to Him, either.

In Mark 16, we have the story of the two men on the road to Emmaus who could not recognize the Lord because it says that *"He appeared in a different form to two of them"* (see Mark 16:12). He obviously did this purposely so that they would recognize Him after the Spirit, and not just appearance. It is also likely that the main reason why we often fail to recognize Him when He tries to draw near to us is that He often comes to us in forms that we are not used to. If we are a Baptist, He may come to us as a Pentecostal. If we are a Charismatic, He may come to us as a Baptist, and so on. He is continually trying to break down the barriers of our religious racism.

Racism is born from the two great evils of pride and fear. It is an ultimate form of pride when we believe we are better than others because of our race. Religious racism is the belief that we are better than others because we are part of a certain denomination or movement. As James 4:6 declares, *"God is opposed to the proud, but gives grace to the humble."* Such pride can be one of the most destructive forces in our lives. It will also turn us into one of those whom the Lord referred to as "goats," because we will refuse to open our hearts to those who are different from us. Racism can be rooted in either pride or fear, but both are evil, and both are contrary to the love of God that is the foundation of all truth.

# *Points to Ponder*

The Lord so loves diversity that He made every snowflake different.

You should love diversity, and yet respect order and purpose. When properly combined, you will be much closer to becoming like Him.

If you have His heart for diversity and creativity, whenever you meet someone who is different, you will be open and expectant of learning something, not closed and fearful.

Racism is rooted in either pride or fear, but both are evil, and both are contrary to the love of God that is the foundation of all truth.

God is continually trying to break down the barriers of religious racism.

# *Words of Wisdom*

If we want the meaning and the worth and the beauty and the power of the cross of Christ to be seen and loved in our churches, and if the design of the death of His Son is not only to reconcile us to God but to reconcile alienated ethnic groups to each other in Christ, then will we not display and magnify the cross of Christ better by more and deeper and sweeter ethnic diversity and unity in our worship and life?

—John Piper, *Brothers, We Are Not Professionals*[1]

We all should know that diversity makes for a rich tapestry, and we must understand that all the threads of the tapestry are equal in value no matter what their color.

—Maya Angelou

Ultimately, America's answer to the intolerant man is diversity, the very diversity which our heritage of religious freedom has inspired.

—Robert F. Kennedy

# My Wisdom Keys

_____

_____

_____

_____

_____

_____

_____

_____

_____

_____

_____

_____

_____

_____

_____

# 33

# *Wisdom of Marriage*

As soon as the man saw the woman, his heart leapt and he knew she was the one! The man looked at the woman and was charged, but it did not appear to have done the same for Eve. Men tend to be stimulated more by sight than women. Just looking at Eve was enough to convince Adam, but just looking at Adam probably did not do much for Eve. However, the words that Adam spoke probably did mean something to her.

God created romance and sex, and both are to be a wonderful and intimate expression of love between a man and woman. However, He created humankind to be body, soul, and spirit. Romance was created to be more than sex. It was to be a union of spirit, soul, and body, in that order. If the order is reversed so that the union of bodies is esteemed first, then it is unlikely that the union of spirit and soul will take place, and the loneliness will continue.

[The following excerpts are adapted from *Unshakable Faith*.]

# Wisdom of Marriage Reflections

THIS is why the Lord created the institution of marriage, and sanctioned that sex outside of marriage is a sin against Him. It is a sin against the very nature of man that God created. Humankind was created to be creatures of lofty intelligence and spirituality. They were also physical creatures who were "wonderfully made." The Lord wanted the crown of His creation to be whole and fulfilled on all three levels, and if humankind started esteeming the physical above the others, a basic perversion of their nature would occur. Therefore, sex was to be an expression of the love and union of spirit and soul. Only as it was this expression of love and union would it truly be fulfilling, and remain the high and lofty expression that it was intended to be. There is a spiritual sensuality that can be released through the love and union of spirit and soul that physical sensuality can never compare with.

In the first meeting of Adam and Eve, Adam was immediately convinced that they were right for each other. It appears that Eve may have taken a little more convincing. She was different, and probably needed to be touched more in her soul and spirit before she could be fully convinced. God made women this way to call men to higher levels of experience. Women do tend to be more spiritually oriented, and often interpreted as more emotional, because they tend to be more in touch with their spiritual senses.

Since the Fall, women have been blamed because Eve was deceived and offered the forbidden fruit to Adam. However, this implies that Adam was not deceived, and sinned even though he knew what he was doing. That is far more sinister. Why did Adam follow Eve that way? It was probably because she had been created to help Adam reach higher realms of spirituality, and Adam had already learned to follow her in this. It is basic to the devil's strategy to turn our strengths into weaknesses and use them against us. He seldom tries to stop someone from doing what they are called to do. He learned in the beginning that it is far more effective to get behind them and push them too far.

Understanding the foundations of our nature, temptation, and the perversion of that nature is important for us to understand redemption and the process of restoration. When we are fully restored, the relationship between men and God, men and women, and men and women with the creation will all be part of a glorious paradise again.

# *Points to Ponder*

God created romance and sex, and both are to be a
wonderful and intimate expression of love between
a man and woman.

Sex is to be an expression of the love and union
of spirit and soul.

It is basic to the devil's strategy to turn your strengths into
weaknesses and use them against you.

Understanding the foundations of your nature, temptation,
and the perversion of that nature is important for you to
understand redemption and the process of restoration.

When we are fully restored, the relationship between men
and God and all of creation will all be part of a
glorious paradise again.

# *Words of Wisdom*

Diane was born on Sunday, July 23, 1967, and she died on Sunday, January 16, 2005. It was between those two Sundays that the woman I loved more than anything lived an extraordinary, but abbreviated life.

—Joseph W. Walker III, *Life Between Sundays*[1]

Everyone has some negative legacy that was passed down from previous generations, but you can absolutely take a stand and prevent it from being passed on any further. That's what we've done with our children, and so can you.

—Dani Johnson, *Grooming the Next Generation for Success*[2]

God is more interested in our being right with Him than He is in our being happy in our marriages! Being "right" with Him means getting our sin to the surface where it can be repented of.

—Carl Hampsch, *Opposites Attract*[3]

I can tell you without any fear of contradiction or oversimplification that the root cause of all marriage conflicts is selfishness. I can say that because there's probably no better practical synonym for the concept of sin than selfishness. Sin (i.e., selfishness) is at the heart of all marriage problems.

—Lou Priolo, *The Complete Husband*[4]

# MY WISDOM KEYS

_____

_____

_____

_____

_____

_____

_____

_____

_____

_____

_____

_____

# 34

# *Wisdom and Communication*

It is interesting to note that Adam and Eve did not think it was strange that a serpent spoke to them. From this we can deduce that before the Fall, man could communicate freely with the creatures, and they with him. The Fall caused the corruption of one of man's greatest gifts: the gift of communication.

It is now estimated that even the greatest human genius only uses about 10 percent of his brain. Why has the other 90 percent become dormant? What was it used for in the beginning? It is also interesting that people now live an average of less than 10 percent as long as the first humans. As humans' life spans shrank proportionately, did our mental capacity do so as well?

[The following excerpts are adapted from *Unshakable Faith*.]

# Wisdom and Communication Reflections

ADAM and Eve fell to sin and death because they listened to the wrong voice, the voice of the serpent. The devil does still speak to us and tries to deceive us so that we will give ourselves to sin and rebellion. We must challenge every voice that seeks to lead us into beliefs or actions that contradict God's Word. To counter this, we must develop our own ability to hear the Lord, to understand what He is saying, and to obey His voice.

Those who do not know God believe that it is a form of insanity to think that you have heard the voice of God. However, the Scriptures testify that we are not truly the Lord's sheep unless we know His voice, as we read in John 10:4-5 where the Lord refers to Himself as the good Shepherd:

> *When he puts forth all his own, he goes ahead of them,*
> *and the sheep follow him because they know his voice.*
> *A stranger they simply will not follow, but will flee from*
> *him, because they do not know the voice of strangers.*

The Lord did not say that the lambs knew His voice but, rather, the sheep. Sheep will follow their shepherd while the lambs will follow the sheep. Likewise, the spiritually young usually do need to follow more mature believers until they have grown to know the Lord's voice for themselves. However, it should be the goal of every believer to know the Lord's voice, and be able to quickly and easily distinguish His voice from all the other voices in the world.

Many who claim to be believers assert that the Lord no longer speaks because He has given us the Bible, but the Bible itself refutes this false doctrine. We are told that the Lord never changes, and that He *"is the same yesterday and today and forever"* (Heb. 13:8). He is not an author who just wrote one book and then retired! He is alive and still relates to His people personally in the same ways that He always has.

The Bible is a wonderful gift, and should always be the basis of all doctrine and teaching. However, the Lord does not just relate to His people as the Teacher. He is also our Shepherd, and the sheep follow Him *because they know His voice* (see John 10:4). He is also the Prophet, and He still speaks through His people.

# *Points to Ponder*

The Fall caused the corruption of one of humankind's greatest gifts: the gift of communication.

Adam and Eve fell to sin and death because they listened to the wrong voice, the voice of the serpent.

The devil still speaks to you and tries to deceive you so that you will give yourself to sin and rebellion.

It should be your goal to know the Lord's voice, and be able to quickly and easily distinguish His voice from all of the other voices in the world.

God is alive and still relates to His people personally in the same ways that He always has.

# Words of Wisdom

Your communication will reveal the kind of [person] you really are, because what comes out of your mouth is usually what's in your heart. If you truly desire to exemplify Christ you will seek to become a good communicator. Everything that Jesus Christ communicated was holy, clear, purposeful and timely.

—Stuart Scott, *The Exemplary Husband*[1]

The problem with communication...is the *illusion* that it has been accomplished.

—George Bernard Shaw

Good communication is as stimulating as black coffee, and just as hard to sleep after.

—Anne Morrow Lindbergh

*For He whom God has sent speaks the words of God; for He gives the Spirit without measure* (John 3:34).

# MY WISDOM KEYS

_____

_____

_____

_____

_____

_____

_____

_____

_____

_____

_____

_____

_____

_____

# 35

## Wisdom, Not Jealousy

The first two sons born to the first man and woman had a striking difference in their natures. Just as the Lord made men and women different, He created every individual to be unique. He obviously loves creativity, but this leads us to one of those ultimate questions. Why does the Church, which represents God to the world, tend to be so boringly uniform? Why does the Church, which is supposed to be one with the Creator, tend to be so void of creativity, prone to follow the trends of the world, and usually only limping along years behind it? Those who know the Creator should be the most creative people on the face of the earth. We must cast off the oppressive yokes of limited vision imposed by counterfeit spiritual authorities that pressure the Church into conformity.

[The following excerpts are adapted from *Unshakable Faith*.]

# *Wisdom, Not Jealousy Reflections*

THE struggle for freedom began among the first two brothers. Jealousy led to oppression. Jealousy is always rooted in insecurity, and it has continually been the source of most human conflicts. We see in Matthew 27:18 and Mark 15:10 that it was because of jealousy that the Lord was delivered to be crucified. We also see repeatedly in the Book of Acts and the apostolic epistles that persecution was often motivated by jealousy.

We are told in James 3:16, *"For where jealousy and selfish ambition exist, there is disorder and every evil thing."* The true root of almost every division within the Church is jealousy. Men may use differences in doctrines and other things as excuses, but at the root of them will usually be jealousy. It is the root of almost every human conflict, and is the source of the stifling oppression that seeks to crush uniqueness and creativity. We must learn to recognize and repent of this evil in our own lives and resist the influence it seeks to impose on us through others.

The root of jealousy that was manifested in Cain can be traced to his occupation. Cain was a tiller of the ground, which speaks of earthly mindedness. The ground had been cursed so that it would only bear fruit by sweat, which speaks of human effort, or our own works. This is fine for farmers, but Cain tried to offer the fruit of his own works to the Lord, which will never be an acceptable offering to Him. As Paul said in Acts 17:25, *"Nor is He served by human hands."*

Abel offered a blood sacrifice, which God accepted. This was a prophecy of the blood sacrifice of Jesus that would alone be an acceptable offering to God. That the sacrifice was offered by the younger son was also a prophecy that it would be the "last Adam" who would make the sacrifice acceptable to God. From the very beginning, the Lord made a provision for the redemption of the Fallen world, and also from the very beginning, prophetic actions point us to Jesus and the redemption of the cross.

# *Points to Ponder*

Those who know the Creator should be the most creative people on the face of the earth.

Jealousy is always rooted in insecurity, and it has continually been the source of most human conflicts.

The true root of almost every division within the Church is jealousy.

You must learn to recognize and repent of jealousy and resist the influence it seeks to impose on you through others.

From the very beginning, the Lord made a provision for your redemption through Jesus.

# *Words of Wisdom*

The jealous are troublesome to others, but a torment to themselves.

—William Penn, *Some Fruits of Solitude*[1]

*For he knew that because of envy they had handed Him over* (Matthew 27:18).

*For he was aware that the chief priests had handed Him over because of envy* (Mark 15:10).

Denominations and congregations celebrate the varieties of gifts at their best. But when we add on the ism to those perfectly good nouns, we produce the same old legal-ism that declares that it is not who you know but what you have mastered that qualifies you for the abundant life Christ died to bring.

—James Wilson, *Living as Ambassadors of Relationships*[2]

Envy is not a synonym for jealousy. Synonyms can be used interchangeably; envy and jealousy can't. If you don't believe me, try substituting the word "envious" for "jealous" in the phrase: "For I the Lord your God am a jealous God." Jealousy is possessive and protective; it can be good or bad. God's jealousy—His possessiveness of His people—is a good thing; it protects us from being plucked out of His hand.

—Carol J. Ruvolo, "Envy and Kindness"[3]

_____

_____

_____

_____

_____

_____

_____

_____

_____

_____

_____

_____

_____

_____

# 36

# *Wisdom, Sacrifice, and the Cross*

Unfortunately, cults and satanic worshipers seem to understand the basic principle of the spiritual power of sacrifice better than most Christians do. A remarkable biblical example of this is found in Second Kings 3:26-27. Sacrifice has power.

As the Scriptures declare, all of creation was made for the Son and through Him, and in Him all things hold together (see Col. 1:16-17). There is nothing in this universe as precious as the Son of God. Nothing greater could be sacrificed. That is why the cross is the very power of God (see 1 Cor. 1:18).

[The following excerpts are adapted from *An Enduring Vision*.]

# Wisdom, Sacrifice, and the Cross Reflections

**T**HERE is no power greater in this universe than what is available to us through the cross of Jesus. If the Passover sacrifice of lambs, which was only a type or a prophecy of the coming cross of Jesus, could set Israel free from the most powerful empire on earth at the time, how much more can the actual cross of Jesus set us free from our bondage?

All the combined power of all the armies on earth could not compare with a single drop of the blood of Jesus. That power is available to us at the cross. That is why it only takes faith the size of a single mustard seed to move a mountain! So why does our faith seem to fail us? The reason our "faith" falls short of accomplishing much is that we almost always reduce it to *faith in our faith*, rather than faith in the cross of Jesus.

Just as the purpose of the power of God as demonstrated through Moses was to first set Israel free, we often want to do great exploits with our faith before we have been delivered from our sin. As Christians we may remain in bondage to evil passions, evil desires, and the evil ways of this present evil age. However, if we do, we can never say that we have not been offered the power to be set free from them.

For Christians to say they do not have the power to overcome the sin and evil of their heart is to say that the evil is more powerful than the cross, which is an obvious insult to the cross. The power to be free has been offered to us. We can reject it, but we can never say that it was not available to us. If we remain under the power of sin, it is our choice, because we choose sin over freedom. That is proof of whom we really love and whom we really serve.

There are a host of false doctrines that seek to turn believers away from the power of the cross, proclaiming that it is not possible to be free from the sin and evil passions of this world. Some seek to replace the cross of Jesus with human penitence. The devil knows well that these frivolous attempts to pay the price for our own sins are a profound affront to the cross of Jesus. Such foolishness actually empowers human sin by feeding human selfishness.

The cross of Jesus is enough, and it alone can set us free.

# *Points to Ponder*

There is no power greater in this universe than what is available to you through the cross of Jesus.

All the combined power of all of the armies on earth could not compare with a single drop of the blood of Jesus. That power is available to you at the cross.

You have the power to overcome the sin and evil of your heart because of the cross.

The devil knows that frivolous attempts to pay the price for your own sins are affronts to the cross of Jesus.

Don't empower sin by feeding human selfishness.

# Words of Wisdom

For my own part, I have never ceased to rejoice that God has appointed me to such an office. People talk of the sacrifice I have made in spending so much of my life in Africa. Is that a sacrifice which brings its own blest reward in healthful activity, the consciousness of doing good, peace of mind, and a bright hope of a glorious destiny hereafter? Away with the word *sacrifice*. Say rather it is a *privilege*. Anxiety, sickness, suffering, or danger, now and then, with a forgoing of the common conveniences and charities of this life, may make us pause, and cause the spirit to waver, and the soul to sink; but let this only be for a moment. All these are nothing when compared with the glory which shall be revealed in and for us. I never made a sacrifice.

—David Livingstone

If God would grant us the vision, the word *sacrifice* would disappear from our lips and thoughts; we would hate the things that seem now so dear to us; our lives would suddenly be too short; we would despise time-robbing distractions and charge the enemy with all our energies in the name of Christ. May God help us to judge ourselves by the eternities that separate the Aucas from a comprehension of Christmas, and Him, who, though He was rich, yet for our sakes became poor so that we might, through His poverty, be made rich. Lord God, speak to my own heart and give me to know Thy holy will and the joy of walking in it. Amen.

—Nate Saint, written just before he was martyred by the Auca Indians in South America

*For the word of the cross is foolishness to those who are perishing, but to us who are being saved it is the power of God* (1 Corinthians 1:18).

# MY WISDOM KEYS

_____

_____

_____

_____

_____

_____

_____

_____

_____

_____

_____

_____

_____

# 37

# *Wisdom to Dream of Heaven*

Genesis 28:12-17 tells of a remarkable experience that Jacob had, which is also relevant to us today. The first point to observe is that, to Jacob, the dream was real. Dreams can be a window into the heavenly realm. For this reason dreams have been one of the primary ways the Lord has spoken to His people from the beginning. In Acts 2:17, we see it will continue to be one of the primary ways that He speaks to us at the end. It is becoming increasingly crucial as we proceed toward the end of this age that we understand dreams, are able to distinguish which are from the Lord and which are not, and are able to interpret them.

[The following excerpts are adapted from *An Enduring Vision*.]

# Wisdom to Dream of Heaven Reflections

**T**HE second point is that Jacob saw a gate into Heaven, and when he saw into Heaven he was given a revelation of his purpose on earth. The purpose of all true prophetic revelations is to have His Kingdom come to earth and His will be done *"on earth as it is in heaven"* (Matt. 6:10). True prophetic revelation will always be practical.

The third point is that the word translated "angel" in Genesis 28 is the Hebrew word *mal'ak*. The messengers who are to ascend and descend upon this ladder are not just angelic beings, but God's messengers, which we are called to be.

The fourth point involves the reason that messengers of God are called to ascend and descend upon the ladder. A primary purpose of prophetic revelation is to call the Church to rise above the earth and to dwell in the heavenly realm now. Just as the revelation to Jacob spoke of the land upon which he was lying, the purpose of our entering into the heavenly realm is to bring the blessings and benefits of that realm to earth.

For the next point we need to read John 1:49-51:

*Nathanael answered Him, "Rabbi, You are the Son of God; You are the King of Israel." Jesus answered and said to him, "Because I said to you that I saw you under the fig tree, do you believe? You will see greater things than these." And He said to him, "Truly, truly, I say to you,*

*you will see the heavens opened and the angels of God ascending and descending on the Son of Man."*

Here we see that Jesus is Jacob's ladder. The rungs on the ladder are the progressive revelations of Jesus. When we come to know Him as our Savior, we take a step. When we come to know Him as our Lord, we take another. When we come to know Him as the Lord above all lords, we go higher. When we see Him as the One through whom and for whom all things were made, we take another step, and so on.

The Lord is calling us to come up to where He sits. Just as there seems to be no limit to the expanding universe that we can see, neither is there a limit to the One we can see only with the eyes of our heart. He has not limited how far we can go, even to sitting with Him on His throne.

# *Points to Ponder*

Dreams can be a window into the heavenly realm.

Dreams have been one of the primary ways the Lord has spoken to His people from the beginning.

The purpose of all true prophetic revelations is to have His Kingdom come to earth and His will be done on earth as it is in Heaven.

When you come to know Him as your Savior, you take a step. When you come to know Him as your Lord, you take another.

The Lord is calling you to come up to where He sits.

# *Words of Wisdom*

For the Christian, heaven is where Jesus is. We do not need to speculate on what heaven will be like. It is enough to know that we will be forever with Him. When we love anyone with our whole hearts, life begins when we are with that person; it is only in their company that we are really and truly alive. It is so with Christ. In this world our contact with Him is shadowy, for we can only see through a glass darkly. It is spasmodic, for we are poor creatures and cannot live always on the heights. But the best definition of it is to say that heaven is that state where we will always be with Jesus, and where nothing will separate us from Him anymore.

—William Barclay, *The Gospel of John*

I had rather be in hell with Christ, than be in heaven without Him.

—Martin Luther

*"And it shall be in the last days," God says, "that I will pour forth of My spirit on all mankind; and your sons and your daughters shall prophesy, and your young men shall see visions, and your old men shall dream dreams"* (Acts 2:17).

# MY WISDOM KEYS

_____

_____

_____

_____

_____

_____

_____

_____

_____

_____

_____

_____

_____

_____

_____

_____

# 38

# *Wisdom of the Holy Spirit*

As the Spirit is poured out on all of the Body, the result will be prophetic revelations such as dreams, visions, and prophecies. This is why it is so crucial that we learn to discern, interpret, and apply them properly. If you have not already started having such experiences, you will, as the prophecies from Joel and Acts make clear.

[The following excerpts are adapted from *An Enduring Vision*.]

# Wisdom of the Holy Spirit Reflections

IF we are going to dwell in the heavenly realm, we must learn the language of the Spirit, which is very different from human language and includes, not only prophecies, but also dreams and visions. With the Lord, the saying "a picture is worth a thousand words" is even more true. The Lord conveys many of His messages to us in pictures. These do not just convey facts or commands; they also reveal His heart and the reasons behind His actions (as prophecies do), so we can be in unity with Him.

There are still many who believe that since we have the Scriptures, we have no need for the Lord to speak to us. We certainly do not want to in any way detract from the immeasurable value of the Scriptures. But this kind of argument is not only in conflict with the teaching of the Scriptures from beginning to end, it also misses something fundamental in the very relationship between God and His people. The Church is called to be Christ's Bride. How would any bride feel if on her wedding day her bridegroom handed her a book saying, "I wrote this for you so I will not have to speak to you again."

The Scriptures are complete and are alone the basis for our doctrine. The gift of prophecy is not given to establish doctrine—we have the Scriptures for that. Prophecy is given for revealing the strategic will of the Lord in specific situations. Even those who claim they do not believe that the Lord speaks to us in this way will usually say they are in ministry because the Lord spoke to them in some way.

However, prophecy is not just about the strategic will of the Lord. The quality of any relationship will be measured by the quality of the communication. Much of what the Lord is saying to His people is simply "love talk," by which He is wooing us closer to Himself.

It is certainly important for us to be solidly established in sound biblical doctrine. It is important for us to know the plan of God and the strategic will of God for our own lives. Even so, there is nothing in life more important than getting closer to Him and abiding in Him day by day.

# *Points to Ponder*

As the Holy Spirit is poured out on all of the Body, there will be prophetic revelations such as dreams, visions, and prophecies.

Have you started having such experiences as the prophecies from Joel and Acts make clear?

The Lord conveys many of His messages to you in pictures that reveal His heart and the reasons behind His actions.

Prophecy is given for revealing the strategic will of the Lord in specific situations.

There is nothing in life more important than getting closer to Him and abiding in Him day by day.

# *Words of Wisdom*

Watch out for any ministry or person who claims to be led by the Holy Spirit but acts contrary to the Word of God. And beware of any movement or group whose focus is the Holy Spirit. The Holy Spirit points not to Himself but to Jesus Christ.

—George Sweeting, *Who Said That?*[1]

*Or do you not know that your body is a temple of the Holy Spirit who is in you, whom you have from God, and that you are not your own?* (1 Corinthians 6:19)

- The Holy Spirit as the Spirit of Power helpeth our infirmity in prayer.

- The Holy Spirit as the Spirit of Life ends our deadness in prayer.

- The Holy Spirit as the Spirit of Wisdom delivers us from ignorance in this holy art of prayer.

- The Holy Spirit as the Spirit of Fire delivers us from coldness in prayer.

- The Holy Spirit as the Spirit of Might comes to our aid in our weakness as we pray.

—Leonard Ravenhill

*Now may the God of hope fill you with all joy and peace in believing, so that you will abound in hope by the power of the Holy Spirit* (Romans 15:13).

# My Wisdom Keys

_____

_____

_____

_____

_____

_____

_____

_____

_____

_____

_____

_____

_____

_____

_____

# 39

## *Wisdom and Loyalty*

Because Robert E. Lee esteemed loyalty to his native state of Virginia above some of the basic principles in which he believed, his misplaced loyalty cost multitudes their lives. Many Christians likewise justify actions that are in basic conflict with the Scriptures and the nature of the Lord they claim to serve. They esteem loyalty to their nation, denomination, or other institution, above the basic principles of the faith.

This is not to in any way imply that loyalty to our nation, denomination, or even our company, is wrong. Loyalty is a noble characteristic found in every truly noble soul. However, we must esteem loyalty to our God above all of these or they have become idols. We must always obey God rather than people when there is a conflict between the two, if He is truly our Lord.

[The following excerpts are adapted from *An Enduring Vision*.]

# Wisdom and Loyalty Reflections

**M**ANY have probably compromised the basic tenets of our faith in this way because they do not really know the principles of the faith, having failed to search the Scriptures for themselves. Every nation that goes to war will try to fan the flames of religious zeal on behalf of their cause. Few things provide greater motivation in drumming up the devotion and sacrifice required to win a war. Many are duped for the cause of evil in this way. What can we do about it?

If you are wondering where this is leading, I am actually trying to keep you from taking "the mark of the beast." Many have simplistically thought that it will be easy to refuse the mark. They earnestly believe that, if anyone tries to put it on their forehead or hand (especially a mark that includes the number 666), they simply will not take it.

However, a study quickly reveals that this mark is far more subtle. It is not just having truth that will keep us from being deceived, but having a love for the truth, which we read about in Second Thessalonians 2:8-12.

Robert E. Lee was a remarkably Christlike man in his daily life and demeanor. He once got down from his horse to minister to a wounded Union soldier who had just cursed him. Several times, his top generals failed to carry out his orders at the most crucial point in several major battles—in two cases probably costing him a decisive victory that could have won the war. Even so, he never publicly berated his subordinates, but took all the blame upon himself. He once got up early to personally serve a meal to a junior officer whom he had misjudged. He refused throughout the war to sleep in anything but a tent, sharing all the same hardships that his soldiers did. While Union soldiers burned fields, farms, and towns throughout the South, Lee severely punished any who damaged the property of his enemies. He also made his generals pay the full price for any provisions they took from farmers.

Loyalty is a wonderful and glorious motivator, but if we are loyal to any person or entity more than we are loyal to the Lord Jesus and His truth, we too, will be in jeopardy of fighting for wrong, regardless of how noble or valiant we are.

# *Points to Ponder*

Many Christians justify actions that are in basic conflict with the Scriptures and the nature of the Lord.

Some Christians esteem loyalty to their nation, denomination, or other institution, above the basic principles of their faith.

Loyalty is a noble characteristic found in every truly noble soul. However, we must esteem loyalty to our God above all of these or they have become idols.

Loyalty is a wonderful and glorious motivator, but if you are loyal to any person or entity more than you are loyal to the Lord Jesus and His truth, you will be in jeopardy of fighting for wrong, regardless of how noble or valiant you are.

# *Words of Wisdom*

*He who pursues righteousness and loyalty finds life, righteousness and honor* (Proverbs 21:21).

The men who followed Him [Jesus] were unique in their generation. They turned the world upside down because their hearts had been turned right side up. The world has never been the same.

—Billy Graham

You can't see who Jesus is. You just have to *know* who He is by the Spirit. If the Spirit doesn't reveal it to you, then you cannot *know*, because God is never recognized, but revealed.

—Noel Jones, *God's Gonna Make You Laugh*[1]

A boy can learn a lot from a dog: obedience, loyalty, and the importance of turning around three times before lying down.

—Robert Benchley

# My Wisdom Keys

# 40

## *Wisdom's Love*

As we are told in First Timothy 1:5, *"The goal of our instruction is love from a pure heart and a good conscience and a sincere faith."* We have discussed our need for power to be witnesses of the God who is all-powerful. We must also understand that God is love and we cannot be His witnesses without love. Our primary goal in life should be the fruit of the Spirit and power. The power of God is the demonstration of His love.

[The following excerpts are adapted from *An Enduring Vision*.]

# Wisdom's Love Reflections

THE Lord did not heal people to reveal His power, but to demonstrate the power of His love for them. If He had wanted to demonstrate His power, He could have done much greater things—like moving mountains, or parting seas, as in Moses' day. He could have stopped the sun, as He did for Joshua, or even written His name across the sky with stars. He used His power for the sake of love. He healed people because He loved them and did not want them to be sick. He healed because healing, redemption, and restoration are His nature—because love is His nature.

As we have discussed, we are the Lord's Body on the earth. He wants to do His works through His people. He does not just want to use us as He might an inanimate object; but He wants us to be in unity with Him. He wants us to have both His mind and His heart. He wants us to feel what He feels for people.

The Lord did some of His greatest miracles, like walking on the water, before only a handful of people. He could have preached His sermons standing on a lake, but He didn't. When He performed miracles it was not for the purpose of getting people's attention. He did it out of obedience to the Father. Over and over, we read that He was moved by compassion because that is what the Father was feeling. We, too, must learn to be moved by what moves God. There is something in us that will want to do the greatest miracles in front of the most people, but when we are mature, our greatest reward is to watch the Lord help others.

Some of the greatest demonstrations of power are not found in merely healing people, but in keeping them well. Certainly, this does not give as much of a "witness" to His power, but it is just as much a demonstration of His power, and maybe an even greater demonstration of His love. The protection of God is no less a miracle. Let us see and acknowledge His works in all things, knowing that:

> *Every good thing given and every perfect gift is from*
> *above, coming down from the Father of lights, with*
> *whom there is no variation or shifting shadow*
> (James 1:17).

# *Points to Ponder*

God is love, and you cannot be His witness without love.

God healed because healing, redemption, and restoration are His nature—because love is His nature.

When Jesus performed miracles, it was not for the purpose of getting people's attention. He did it out of obedience to the Father.

Over and over, Jesus was moved by compassion because that is what the Father was feeling.

You must learn to be moved by what moves God.

# Words of Wisdom

*But now faith, hope, love, abide these three; but the greatest of these is love* (1 Corinthians 13:13).

Love, as distinct from "being in love," is not merely a feeling. It is a deep unity, maintained by the will and deliberately strengthened by habit; reinforced by the grace which both partners ask and receive from God. They can have this love for each other even at those moments when they do not like each other; as you love yourself even when you do not like yourself.

—C.S. Lewis, *Mere Christianity*[1]

To the Christian, love is the works of love. To say that love is a feeling or anything of the kind is really an un-Christian conception of love. That is the aesthetic definition and therefore fits the erotic and everything of that nature. But to the Christian, love is the works of love. Christ's love was not an inner feeling, a full heart and what-not: it was the work of love which was His life.

—Soren Kierkegaard

Joy is love exalted; peace is love in repose; long-suffering is love enduring; gentleness is love in society; goodness is love in action; faith is love on the battlefield; meekness is love in school; and temperance is love in training.

—D.L. Moody

# MY WISDOM KEYS

_____

_____

_____

_____

_____

_____

_____

_____

_____

_____

_____

_____

_____

# Endnotes

**Note:** Short quotes are taken from Grace Quotes; www.thegracetabernacle.org/quotes/grace_qs_bkgrnd.html; www.thinkexist.com; and www.wisdomquotes.com, accessed Dec. 2009–Jan. 2010.

## INTRODUCTION

1.  Rick Joyner, *An Enduring Vision* (Shippensburg, PA: Destiny Image, 2010); *High Calling* (Shippensburg, PA: Destiny Image, 2010); *Overcoming Evil in the Last Days* (Shippensburg, PA: Destiny Image, 2009); *Breaking the Power of Evil* (Shippensburg, PA: Destiny Image, 2008); *Delivered From Evil* (Shippensburg, PA: Destiny Image, 2004); *Unshakable Faith* (Shippensburg, PA: Destiny Image, 2000).

2.  Rick Joyner, *Delivered From Evil* (Shippensburg, PA: Destiny Image, 2004), 15.

## CHAPTER 1

1.  J.L. Dagg, *Manual of Theology* (Gano Books, 1982 edition of original 1857 edition published by The Southern Baptist Publication Society), 86-87.

## CHAPTER 2

1. Myles Munroe, *Wisdom From Myles Munroe* (Shippensburg, PA: Destiny Image, 2010).

2. T.D. Jakes, *Power for Living* (Shippensburg, PA: Destiny Image, 2009), 121.

3. Ché Ahn, *Say Goodbye to Powerless Christianity* (Shippensburg, PA: Destiny Image, 2009), 72.

## CHAPTER 3

1. Kris Vallotton and Bill Johnson, *The Supernatural Ways of Royalty* (Shippensburg, PA: Destiny Image, 2006), 173.

2. Morris Cerullo, *How to Pray* (Shippensburg, PA: Destiny Image, 2004), 89.

3. John Stott, "The Great Commission," in *One Race, One Gospel, One Task,* World Congress on Evangelism, Berlin 1966, Official Reference Volumes, ed. Carl F.H. Henry and W. Stanley Mooneyham (Minneapolis: World Wide Publications, 1967), vol. I, p. 46.

## CHAPTER 4

1. Elmer L. Towns, *Praying the Book of Revelation* (Shippensburg, PA: Destiny Image, 2007), 66.

2. Keith Hudson, *The Cry* (Shippensburg, PA: Destiny Image, 2009), 87.

## CHAPTER 5

1. C.S. Lewis, *Mere Christianity*, 99.

2. Jonathan Welton, *The School of the Seers* (Shippensburg, PA: Destiny Image, 2009), 111.

## CHAPTER 6

1. Scot Anderson, *God Wants You Rich, Not Poor & Struggling* (Shippensburg, PA: Destiny Image, 2009), 69.

2. Noel Jones and Scott Chaplan, *Vow of Prosperity* (Shippensburg, PA: Destiny Image, 2007), 29.

## CHAPTER 7

1. John MacArthur, *Twelve Ordinary Men* (John MacArthur, 2002), 80.

2. Nancy Leigh DeMoss, *Holiness, The Heart God Purifies* (Chicago: Moody Publishers, 2004), 175-176.

## CHAPTER 8

1. Jeff Rostocil, *Unshakable* (Shippensburg, PA: Destiny Image, 2009), 53.

2. Doug Stringer, *Hope for a Fatherless Generation* (Shippensburg, PA: Destiny Image, 2009), 38.

## CHAPTER 9

1. C.H. Spurgeon, *"A Jealous God,"* Sermon 502, March 29, 1863.

2. Danny Silk, *Culture of Honor* (Shippensburg, PA: Destiny Image, 2009), 69.

## CHAPTER 10

1. Mark J. Chironna, *Live Your Dream* (Shippensburg, PA: Destiny Image, 2009), 155.

2. R.C. Sproul, *The Dark Night of the Soul* (Tabletalk, March 2008, Used by Permission).

3. T.D. Jakes, *Wisdom From T.D. Jakes* (Shippensburg, PA: Destiny Image, 2010), 178.

## CHAPTER 11

1. Sinclair B. Ferguson, *Grow in Grace* by permission of Banner of Truth (Carlisle, PA: Banner of Truth, 1989), 33-34.

## CHAPTER 12

1. David E. Taylor, *Face-to-Face Appearances from Jesus* (Shippensburg, PA: Destiny Image, 2009), 101.

2. Delores Winder with Bill Keith, *Surprised by Healing* (Shippensburg, PA: Destiny Image, 2007), 135.

## CHAPTER 13

1. Ruth and Elmer Towns, *How to Build a Lasting Marriage* (Shippensburg, PA: Destiny Image, 2003), 125.

## CHAPTER 14

1. Larry Kreider and Dennis De Grasse, *Supernatural Living* (Shippensburg, PA: Destiny Image, 2009), 52.

2. Ravi Zacharias, *This We Believe* (Grand Rapids, MI: Zondervan, 2000), 33.

## CHAPTER 15

1. Jackie Kendall and Debby Jones, *Lady in Waiting* (Shippensburg, PA: Destiny Image, 2005), 15.

2. Angus N. Hunter, *From Venus to Mars and Back* (Shippensburg, PA: Destiny Image, 2009), 39.

3. Myles Munroe and David Burrows, *Kingdom Parenting* (Shippensburg, PA: Destiny Image, 2007), 15.

## CHAPTER 16

1. Frank Bailey, *Holy Spirit, the Promised One* (Shippensburg, PA: Destiny Image, 1998), 112.

2. John Owen, *Sin and Temptation* (public domain).

3. Jerry Bridges, *Transforming Grace* (Colorado Springs, CO: NavPress, 1991), 198.

## CHAPTER 17

1. Alan Vincent, *The Good Fight of Faith* (Shippensburg, PA: Destiny Image, 2008), 59.

2. Sid Roth and Linda Josef, *Supernatural Healing* (Shippensburg, PA: Destiny Image, 2007), 59.

3. Kris Vallotton, *Developing a Supernatural Lifestyle* (Shippensburg, PA: Destiny Image, 2007), 135.

4. John MacArthur, *Charismatic Chaos* (Grand Rapids, MI: Zondervan, © John MacArthur, 1992), 127-128.

## CHAPTER 18

1. Cal Thomas, "The Authority of the State," (*Tabletalk*, March, 2009), 20. Used by Permission.

2. John Piper, *World,* September 22, 2001.

## CHAPTER 19

1. Philip Graham Ryken, *Is Jesus the Only Way?* (Wheaton, IL: Crossway, 1999), 29.

2. Joel Belz, *World* (November/December 2001).

## CHAPTER 20

1. Faisal Malick, *Positioned to Bless* (Shippensburg, PA: Destiny Image, 2008), 203.

2. Banning Liebscher, *Jesus Culture* (Shippensburg, PA: Destiny Image, 2009), 111.

## CHAPTER 21

1. Morris Cerullo, *You Can Have a New Beginning* (Shippensburg, PA: Destiny Image, 2009), 90.

2. Sir William Blackstone, *Commentaries on the Law of England*, (1765-1769).

3. Kurt Bruner, *The Twilight Phenomenon* (Shippensburg, PA: Destiny Image, 2009), 11.

## CHAPTER 22

1. Bill Johnson, *Strengthen Yourself in the Lord* (Shippensburg, PA: Destiny Image, 2007), 56.

2. Joseph Mattera, *Kingdom Revolution* (Shippensburg, PA: Destiny Image, 2009), 155.

3. Curtis C. Thomas, *Practical Wisdom for Pastors* (Wheaton, IL: Crossway Books, 2001), 209.

## CHAPTER 23

1. Kris Vallotton, *Sexual Revolution* (Shippensburg, PA: Destiny Image, 2008), 86.

2. Harold R. Eberle, *Christianity Unshackled* (Shippensburg, PA: Destiny Image, 2009), 234.

## CHAPTER 24

1. Sid Roth, *The Incomplete Church* (Shippensburg, PA: Destiny Image, 2007), 106.

2. Charles P. Schmitt, *End-Time Truths for End-Time People* (Shippensburg, PA: Destiny Image, 2009), 97.

## CHAPTER 25

1. Elisabeth Elliot, *Discipline: The Glad Surrender* (Ada, MI: Revell, 1982), 74.

## CHAPTER 26

1. Faisal Malick, *The Destiny of Islam in the Endtimes* (Shippensburg, PA: Destiny Image, 2007), 69.

2. Richard Booker, *The Miracle of the Scarlet Thread* (Shippensburg, PA: Destiny Image, 2008), 12.

## CHAPTER 27

1. Elmer L. Towns, *How God Answers Prayer* (Shippensburg, PA: Destiny Image, 2009), 202.

2. T.D. Jakes, *40 Days of Power* (Shippensburg, PA: Destiny Image, 2009), 167.

3. Don Nori, *The Love Shack* (Shippensburg, PA: Destiny Image, 2009), 131.

## CHAPTER 28

1. Donna Scuderi, et al., *Reflections on 90 Minutes in Heaven* (Shippensburg, PA: Destiny Image, 2009), 99.

## CHAPTER 29

1. Terry Nance, *God's Armorbearer* (Shippensburg, PA: Destiny Image, 2004), 142.

2. Bob Lenz, *Grace* (Shippensburg, PA: Destiny Image, 2008), 115.

## CHAPTER 30

1. Mickey Robinson, *The Prophetic Made Personal* (Shippensburg, PA: Destiny Image, 2010), 92.

2. Sharon L. Grant, *Giving Up is Not an Option* (Shippensburg, PA: Destiny Image, 2010), 114.

## CHAPTER 31

1. Francis Schaeffer, *A Christian Manifesto* (Wheaton, IL: Crossway Books, 2005).

2. Mark Van Deman, *A Traveler's Guide to the Spirit Realm* (Shippensburg, PA: Destiny Image, 2007), 48.

## CHAPTER 32

1. John Piper, *Brothers, We Are Not Professionals* (Bethlehem Baptist Church, 2002), 207.

## CHAPTER 33

1. Joseph W. Walker III, *Life Between Sundays* (Shippensburg, PA: Destiny Image, 2009), 28.

2. Dani Johnson, *Grooming the Next Generation for Success* (Shippensburg, PA: Destiny Image, 2009), 40.

3. Carl Hampsch, *Opposites Attract* (Shippensburg, PA: Destiny Image, 2007), 37.

4. Lou Priolo, *The Complete Husband* (Calvary Press, 1999).

## CHAPTER 34

1. Stuart Scott, *The Exemplary Husband* (Focus Publishing, 2000), 229.

## CHAPTER 35

1. William Penn, *Some Fruits of Solitude*, 1693.

2. James Wilson, *Living as Ambassadors of Relationships* (Shippensburg, PA: Destiny Image, 2008), 51.

3. Carol J. Ruvolo, "Envy and Kindness," *Tabletalk* (May 2008), 21. Used by Permission.

## CHAPTER 38

1. George Sweeting, *Who Said That?* (Chicago, IL: Moody Press, 1995), 236.

## CHAPTER 39

1. Noel Jones, *God's Gonna Make You Laugh* (Shippensburg, PA: Destiny Image, 2007), 94.

## CHAPTER 40

1.  C.S. Lewis, *Mere Christianity*, 99.